COLLEGE ·MATCH·

A Blueprint for Choosing the Best School for You

Fifteenth Edition
Revised and Updated

By Steven R. Antonoff, Ph.D.

College Match
A Blueprint for Choosing the Best School for You

Fifteenth Edition
By Steven R. Antonoff, Ph.D.

Book Design by I/O Designs
Cover and chapter Illustrations by Milan Glosic

Address correspondence to:
EDUconsultingMedia
info@EDUconsultingMedia.com
EDUconsultingMedia.com

ISBN   978-1-7335784-2-4
PRINTED IN THE UNITED STATES OF AMERICA

Dedication

In memory of my mom, dad, sister, and brother. My years with some of you were few but my years with all of you were formative in terms of mindset and conduct. As I remember them here, I challenge you to tell your loved ones—family and friends—how much they mean to you.

Contents

Preface
Introduction to the Fifteenth Edition

Revising **College Match** is always great fun. It's fun because these are changing times in the college admission world, and I'm eager to share current insights and perspectives with readers. For this edition of Match, I made revisions based on three elements: 1) changes in college admission, such as the trend toward test scores being optional in the admission process; 2) changes in the perspectives of prospective college students, to some extent the result of learning experiences that resulted from COVID; and 3) changes in society that affects college planning, such as the increased sensitivity to the cost and value of a college education.

The value of being a practicing counselor is that I can use, test, and refine the information and materials in this book. I've done that extensively for this edition. This book intends to provide perspective and guidance to college shoppers. As it has been in editions of this book spanning 30 years, my goal in this edition is to provide a framework on which to base solid college choices.

Specifically, four principles guided the writing of this book:

- *All students, regardless of grades or test scores, have colleges from which to choose.* Many more quality colleges (as measured by factors such as faculty and student excellence, success at career preparation, and facilities) exist now than when this book was first published. Now more than ever, great colleges are out there waiting to be found. Students merely need to seize the opportunity by taking the time to search. Through this book, along with proper guidance and support, students will find colleges where they can be successful. While it is true that college admission has become much more competitive in recent years, it is also true that the collegiate opportunities in the United States and around the world are limitless.
- *There is a sequence of steps that, if followed, will lead to solid, suitable college choices.* This book is organized around those steps. Systematically moving from one stage to the next will lead to self-knowledge and college awareness. These "awarenesses" provide the foundation on which students should base their college choice.
- *The college choice process neither has to be nor is, inherently stressful.* Over the last several years, anxiety, even panic, about selecting a college has increased. Some of that stress comes from false assumptions about the nature of college admission. Once students and their families replace the quest for "the best college" with one focusing on "the best-fit college," the level of tension is significantly reduced. While this book covers both "getting in" and "fitting in," it focuses on "fitting in" because I feel this should be the primary emphasis throughout the college selection process. "Fitting in" is the largest contributor to creating a good college experience.

1

- *Finding a college builds essential, lifelong skills in taking initiative, making decisions, and assuming responsibility.* Each revision of *College Match* gives me more of a chance to observe the lessons college planning provides. *College Match* encourages students to take the lead in their college planning and to grow as a result. For many students, choosing a college is their first real-life choice. By making difficult decisions during the college choice process and accepting the consequences of their decisions, students gain self-understanding and an understanding of how life works. This knowledge will stand them in good stead long after their college careers have ended.

Specific Changes in This Edition

The Self-Survey for the College Bound has been completely revised. The revision includes exciting new categories (among them, "Tenacity," Emotional Vocabulary," "Growth Mindset," and "Academic Ownership") while preserving the categories that have proven to most helpful, such as "Academic/Social Balance" and "Participant Learner." The Self-Survey was also shortened to be easier to take and to score. The number of students taking this Survey via this book or my website (schoolbuff.com) has increased dramatically in recent years and is currently taken by hundreds of students weekly. I'm very encouraged by the changes to this popular part of the book and am eager for your feedback.

Two other surveys have been revised. *The Audit of College Success Traits* asks students to evaluate themselves on 13 traits correlated with college success. Traits include such vital elements as motivation, adaptability, resourcefulness, and even intercultural curiosity. This Survey, *Appendix I*, is the revision of the Self-Knowledge Questionnaire from previous editions.

The College Planning Values Assessment (Appendix H) now includes a more explicit group of values and new, up-to-date descriptions of the meaning of each. I believe getting to what a student is looking for in a college by identifying values can be very useful when used with other worksheets and other surveys in this book. Values provide another window into student thinking, a window I think can be clear and free of the presuppositions of differentiating features such as size, location, and academic major.

New resources included in this latest *College Match* point you to the best strategies for finding colleges, managing costs, applying to college, and tackling every other aspect of college search and selection. In addition, updates and revisions have been made to each chapter in the interest of keeping the book accurate, timely, and easy to use.

The essence of *College Match* and its general parameters remain much the same as in its first edition. Since its inception, a hallmark of *College Match* has been its interactive nature, grounded in a series of worksheets that prompt you to examine who you are and what matters to you. Students who actively participate in choosing their college are likely to make better, more satisfying decisions. The Self-Survey, the central component of *Chapter 2*, is

DREAM JOB THANKS TO CHOOSING A GREAT FIT COLLEGE!

widely used by high school counselors nationwide and remains one of the few attempts to systematically explore the variables that students should consider as they begin their college search. As in the past, several of the worksheets from the book can also be found on my website, schoolbuff.com.

Overall, *College Match* offers you encouragement (laced with realism) to keep you going throughout the college choice process. When you are empowered to know that you have real options from which to choose your future, you will feel more confident and optimistic.

As you begin choosing colleges, I hope you do so with openness and enthusiasm. I also hope you will know the power of choice, and with it, you'll discover schools where the best in you will be revealed. I welcome your feedback and encourage you to e-mail me at info@EDUconsultingMedia.com

Steven R. Antonoff, Ph.D.
info@EDUconsultingMedia.com
Denver, Colorado
January, 2022

To Parents
How to Use This Book

This book is written for students because I believe students should assume responsibility for the college search. But I am sensitive to the depth of parental concern that surrounds the college selection process, and so this book is also meant to assist parents in their important role, too. This is not the easiest time to have a student embarking on her or his college journey. Parents of students in this generation are obliged to pay steep college prices at the same time as they are juggling other needs, such as care for elderly parents. The following tips will guide you through these pages.

Parents should begin by reading **Chapters 1, 4**, and **10**, three chapters that offer clear-eyed perspectives on the college search. You can assist your student by encouraging him or her to move sequentially through the chapters. The chapters are organized according to the way the college planning process most logically unfolds. Students should read one chapter at a time, completing any worksheets in that chapter. **Chapters 2, 3**, and **4** present the most central material, and thus more time should be spent on them. Of course, there may be reasons to alter the order. If, for example, you are planning to visit college campuses, you should read **Chapter 6** immediately. If your student is worried about college essays, he or she will find help in **Chapter 7. College Match** includes thirteen worksheets, each building on the preceding one. Parents can review the worksheets after each has been completed by the student, adding insights as necessary.

Each worksheet has a specific purpose. For example, **Worksheet 2** enables the student to better understand himself or herself as an upcoming college student. **Worksheet 5** delineates the factors your student believes to be important in choosing a college. **Worksheet 5** should be shared and discussed as a family, and you should not hesitate to add factors you feel should be considered in the process of college selection. Some of the worksheets are personal and ask the student to probe his or her background and readiness for college. Such self-assessment can be difficult, and some students feel awkward about sharing these kinds of personal insights with anyone, including parents. But a nonjudgmental attitude and trust will go a long way toward better communication.

You can also alert your student to the revised surveys included at the end of the book. **Appendix H, College Planning Values Assessment**, asks students to explore the "real" reasons for going to college. They are asked to determine whether "to learn about different cultures, peoples, backgrounds" is more or less important when going to college as, "to have a fresh start where no one knows me." Such value decisions can help in determining collegiate environments that will best fulfill those goals. **Appendix I, Audit of College Success Traits,** can assist students in pinpointing readiness for college. The Audit asks students to assess themselves on traits found to be essential to success in college, traits like time management, self-advocacy, and resourcefulness.

You may find the following general guidelines/suggestions useful in maximizing use of *College Match*:

- Students should be encouraged to take the college planning process seriously. It is neither a game nor an exercise. It is a process of thinking, reflecting, researching, and choosing. And it takes time. You can't expect to find a college in a day. It is often laborious, and patience is as necessary here as it was when your child learned to walk or ride a bike.
- Students need to understand the ambiguity that comes with making important decisions. In the case of finding a college, there are no absolutes, few "rights" or "wrongs," and plenty of conflicting information. Parents can assist their student by stressing that a solid college choice will be made if he or she methodically moves from one phase of college identification to the next.
- Parents, like their students, can benefit from the input of experienced counselors. A competent and sensitive counselor brings clarity as well as knowledge to college shopping—and potentially can defuse many familial conflicts as well. Most importantly, the counselor, using the results of the worksheets in this book in combination with information gleaned from years of experience, can point the student toward appropriate colleges for consideration.
- Students are encouraged throughout the book to ask for their parents' opinions and perspectives on different topics. However, you may want to give your student a gentle nudge every now and then to share viewpoints and feelings. I hope the book opens lines of communication and gives both parents and students a useful base of knowledge. During the most important college planning months, you should set aside one hour per week to talk about these issues.
- Throughout the process, attempt to support your son's or daughter's good research skills. Good research includes asking lots of questions, reading, examining oneself, and separating college facts from college lore. Help your student use the resources outlined throughout the book.
- Expect a lot from your student, but be mindful of the difficulty of the teenage years. Adolescence is a time of conflicting feelings and perspectives; teenagers are simultaneously independent and dependent, mature and childlike, all-knowing and yet knowing nothing. They may appear ready to take off for college and at the same time hesitant to leave the security of home and family. Take time to discuss these issues and feelings as they arise.

You have in your hands a blueprint for finding a college. Armed with this information, you should feel empowered to guide your student through the process.

To Counselors
A Note

An experienced counselor's voice helps make this book come alive for the college-bound student, which is why the text often directs the student to seek your counsel. You have gone through the college admission process with numerous students, encouraging their dreams, tempering their ambitions when necessary, sharing in their disappointments and successes. Students benefit from your experience.

In contrast to the outlook presented in many college planning resources, I think the college planning and admission processes are not characterized by easy answers, foolproof formulas, or sure-fire strategies. This is not a book about "gaming" the system. It is also not a book of suggestions for "packaging" an applicant whose only goal is to get into a "name brand" college. Because it provides neither recipes nor guarantees, **College Match** is, I believe, more in keeping with the way the college admission process—and indeed, life itself—unfolds. And, hopefully, it is more in keeping with your own philosophy.

This edition features many new elements intended to help you in your work. The **Self-Survey**, shortened and including many new variables, is perhaps the tool you will find most useful.

I believe this book can be used effectively in busy college counseling offices and in the offices of independent educational consultants. It may serve as a student text for a course in college planning or a series of workshops for juniors and seniors. The material is equally suitable for one-on-one meetings.

Although the topics proceed in sequence, the chapters need not necessarily be used in the order in which they are laid out here; each school counseling office will likely determine the suitability of the chapters (and the worksheets) according to the needs and goals of its own counseling program and the specific population of students it serves.

Perhaps most importantly, this book is designed to maximize the value of your time. Students who use the worksheets and read the text will come to you having reflected on themselves as well as those factors or qualities important in their college choice. They will come to you having given thought to essays or visits or other matters. Having used the worksheets with hundreds of my students, I believe them to be "student-friendly"—with questions, instructions, and interpretations that are self-explanatory and even interesting. When students come to you with this preparation and content, your time with each student can be utilized meaningfully on the most salient college counseling issues.

In addition to the popular (and revised for this edition) *Self-Survey* (*Worksheets 1* and *2*), two other updated surveys appear at the end of the book. *Appendix H, College Planning Values Assessment*, asks students to explore their reasons for going to college. They are asked to determine whether "to learn about different cultures, peoples, backgrounds" is more or less important as they think about an ideal college environment as "to have a fresh start where no one knows me." Such value decisions can help determine collegiate environments that will best fulfill those goals and aid you in your assessment of each candidate. *Appendix I, Audit of College Success Traits*, can assist students in pinpointing readiness for college. The Audit asks students to assess themselves on traits essential to success in college, traits like time management, self-advocacy, and resourcefulness. We tell our students that it's not only about "getting in," but that "being successful" is the ultimate college planning goal. The Audit gives you the chance to discuss readiness with your students and evaluate areas that may need to be honed before the student leaves for college.

I have learned much from the writings and the practices of the many school-based and independent educational counselors with whom I have worked. This book reflects those insights, but my desire to learn continues. As such, I am eager to hear your opinions on the issues raised in the book and how those issues are developed. My e-mail address is found in the *Preface*.

The world of higher education is a rich one. We (public or private school counselors and educational consultants alike) share in the mission of opening up each student's eyes to that world. I hope this book contributes to that mission.

Chapter 1
Your Power to Choose a College

This is a book about choice. Choice is not a simple word. Our lives are filled with an endless array of choices. We ask such questions as: What will I wear today? Should I strive for A's and B's, or am I comfortable with B's and a couple of C's? What will I have for lunch? What courses should I take in school during my senior year? How much commitment do I want to make to sports or to my schoolwork? Will I be in a good or bad mood today? Some choices are relatively simple, others are quite complex. Some affect our lives in a major way, others have few consequences. We make hundreds of choices in the span of even a single day. And not making a choice is a choice as well! The consequences of our choices can be good or bad, positive or negative.

Picking a college is an important choice—perhaps the most important choice you've ever made. Your choice of a college can either be haphazard or considered, a desperate decision at the last minute or a confident acceptance that you have found a place where you can thrive. It all depends on your willingness to devote yourself to the process. If you invest yourself in the search, you will find many schools from which to choose. If you are passive and wait for your counselor or your parents or your best friend or your inbox to bring word of "the perfect school," chances are you'll be disappointed with your ultimate choice.

So much has been written about "getting in" to college that students often seem surprised when the word "choice" is associated with college planning. Today, almost every student, regardless of academic record or family resources, can choose from a wide variety of schools. Perhaps the most difficult task is truly believing that you have the power to do so.

Why is it that students so often believe their choice of colleges is extremely limited? If they haven't received all A's, if their high school classes are not the most competitive offered, or if their scores on SATs or ACTs are below average, they may feel they do not or will not have choices—or at least that they will not get into a "good" college. But these students are wrong, and here's why.

First, as you will see, the definition of a "good" college is terribly subjective and imprecise. A "good" college tends to mean a college that you or your family has heard of. But of the 4,000 or so colleges in the United States, with how many is a typical family really familiar? Very few. The truth is hundreds of good colleges exist. Open yourself up to discovering them.

There is a reverse side to the phenomenon just described. Instead of feeling they have too few choices, some students feel they have too many. Parents are often enthusiastic and thrilled by all these options. A student, however, may be confused and even believe "it would be better if I didn't have a choice." Selecting which colleges to research and apply to can become an overwhelming chore, especially since as a high school student, you may be just acquiring the skills and strategies necessary to make good decisions. At the beginning of the college search, your task may seem overwhelming. But with patience and perseverance, your early frustration will pass, and ultimately, result in better college choices. So don't take the easy way out and just settle for one college or another. Explore.

Your first choice is whether you want a college education. Some students simply assume they will go to college and do not go through the important process of contemplating their lives without a college education. Many business and corporate leaders, to take one segment of society, do not have college degrees and yet they are happy and often financially successful. Be assertive in making your decision to go to college. Articulate why you want to go. It's not enough to say, "I need a college degree to get ahead." (Interestingly, there are some recent studies that dispute this notion.) Instead, you should have the desire to learn; there should be subjects that spark your interest. Articulating the values you see in a college education will enable you to appreciate the benefits such an education could offer you. To aid your thinking, make a list of the outcomes you desire from a college education. Think about the kind of person you want to be as a result of going to college. How will you be different once you have your degree?

Another choice involves deciding whether you want to be a student. Often, students claim they want to go to college, but they don't show the requisite commitment to the academic side of college life. They may picture college as four years of fun and games. While college is filled with a great many social opportunities, college attendance is primarily an academic decision. Are you ready to make a commitment to your studies? Do you have the persistence necessary to be a successful student? Firmly deciding to be a student is important as you contemplate college attendance.

Assuming you're committed to pursuing a college education and to being a student, your next choice is when you want that education to begin. Some students delay the start of their college experience for a year or more to be prepared fully—emotionally as well as intellectually—for the rigors of college education. The so-called "gap year" or "time out" programs are increasingly popular. Many students spend productive years traveling, working, or tackling internships or service projects. And research shows that students who take a year or so between their high school experience and the start of their college career are better prepared to meet the challenges of their college years. Still other students make the choice to begin their education at a two-year college, developing basic skills and confidence, before entering a four-year college. And there are students for whom a trade, vocational, or technical school fits their needs perfectly.

You may feel several emotions as you embark on the task of selecting a college. You may feel happy with your successes in high school and look forward to four wonderful years in college. You may feel regret or anger that you didn't earn higher grades in high school. You may feel terror or panic at the complexity of finding a college that meets your background and personality. You may feel overwhelmed because there are so many colleges to choose from. Or you may feel more than one of these sentiments.

Finding a college should not and need not be traumatic or stressful. You can look at your college choices in a positive or in a negative way. Let's take an example. Suppose Sophie is told she can probably get accepted to 3,900 of the possible 4,000 colleges in the United States. If Sophie is prone to negativism, she may stress out because "Aaagh! I might not get into 100 colleges and what if one of them is my dream school?" On the other hand, Sophie could look at this situation in an appropriate, positive way and say, "Wow, 3,900 colleges want me! That's a lot of schools where I can be successful!" Optimism and perspective are important as you begin to look for a college. Remember, 90% of the colleges in the U.S. accept more than 80% of those who apply.

The diversity and excellence of United States colleges are truly mind-boggling. In fact, our colleges are widely regarded as the best developed in the world. Your investment in the college selection process is the first way to demonstrate your commitment to your future success. It's a unique opportunity to affect your life in a positive way.

College Choice as a Process

Picking a collegiate atmosphere in which to spend four years is best viewed as a process, a series of steps in which each step builds on the previous one. Be sure to take your time and carefully complete each step before moving on to the next. You start with an analysis of yourself as a potential college student. You then review the qualities that will make a college right for you. You next use all of the resources at your disposal to select the colleges to which you will apply. Finally, after hearing from your colleges, you move to the last step: picking the college that you will attend.

The essential premise of this book is that by going through these steps as outlined, you will have excellent colleges from which to choose. But you need to be an active participant in the process and take your selection of a college seriously. You have to be open to valid information from wherever it comes and put aside any stereotypes or preconceived notions about colleges in general or about individual colleges. You need to be organized. (Appendices A-E will help you keep track of important college planning goals.) You need to consult with people who know you and who know colleges and ignore the fad followers and well-meaning but misinformed relatives and friends of friends. The college application process involves making big decisions; while you should direct the total effort, you should also heed the advice of those who are assisting you.

The Lucky 13 Myths about Choosing a College

It's no wonder that the college admission process tends to be a breeding ground for inaccurate perceptions and faulty statements. Every fall, the media ramps up coverage to rank the "best" schools, and Internet forums buzz with anecdotes about "getting in." However, much of this information and even comments from well-meaning friends and family may not be based on facts. Here are thirteen myths that you may come across as you undertake your college selection process.

Myth #1: "Colleges are either good or bad."

Nonsense. By what criterion is a college good or bad? In whose eyes is a college good or bad? Academic quality is not easily assessed and, while some colleges are better known than others, it is not true that these particularly colleges are good and all the rest are bad. The key question should not be, "Is X a good college?" but rather, "Is X a good college for me?" Look for colleges appropriate to your educational background, your goals, your ability, and your personality. Guard against relying on stereotypes in looking for a college.

A "name" school is not necessarily a good school, the "best" colleges are not by definition in the East, and contrary to the popular stereotype, there is great fun to be had at small colleges. Be careful about relying on word of mouth: "Uncle Jack went to Stony Bay College and loved it, so I would like it too." No. Colleges change, and you are not the same person as Uncle Jack. Erase preconceived notions about colleges. Start with a clean slate.

Myth #2: "Future employers and graduate schools give an edge to graduates of prestigious universities."

Not necessarily. As the general level of quality in colleges has risen over the last several decades, and as more and more colleges have distinguished themselves, employers and graduate school admission staffs can no longer rely on the name of a college as the most important selection factor. What will matter is your success in college. So smart students are matching themselves to colleges where they have the potential to make good grades and contribute positively to campus life. These students, having achieved distinguished records in college, are highly sought by company recruiters, graduate schools, and professional schools. Five years out of college, an individual's own qualities and track record will determine whether she gets a raise. Do Ivy League graduates have a lock on lists of the most successful individuals in our society? The richest? The happiest? The most humanitarian? There is no evidence to suggest any of these are true.

Myth #3: "Colleges always choose the 'best' students."

Nope, not true. As with "good" colleges, "best" students can be hard to define. College admission staffs work long and hard to choose students, but no foolproof or magic formula exists. Many variables come into play during admission decisions: courses taken, scores, grades, extracurricular activities, as well as geography, athletics, and a host of other variables. Admission directors often say that in any given year, if they were to go back and make their decisions all over again with the same candidate pool, they would often choose different students to receive letters of admission. So students should be certain their final college list is well balanced in terms of admission difficulty. In other words, students should apply to some colleges where their admission chances are so-so, and some colleges where their chances are quite good.

Myth #4: "Schools that cost more are of higher quality."

Why would this be true? A college education is expensive even at a state university. That one college costs double or triple what another school costs says a lot about the size of its state subsidies and its endowment, very little about the quality of the undergraduate program, and absolutely nothing about whether the college fits you. Many factors go into determining the fee structure at a college. Students should look at how well a school matches their own college selection criteria (see *Chapter 3*) and make few judgments about quality on the basis of cost. If you find a college that offers the right environment for you and costs a bit less, hooray! You are a good researcher of colleges.

Myth #5: "The more rigorous the admission standards, the higher the quality of education."

This relationship is shaky at best. There are many reasons a college might have high admission standards. State universities commonly feel an obligation to in-state students and thus out-of-state admissions may be restricted. A college that has received glowing mention in a national magazine or whose football team has just gone to a Bowl game may see a surge in applications and raise its admission requirements as a result. Some colleges describe their requirements so well that they receive few applications from students who don't meet those requirements; while these colleges may accept a high percentage of students, they maintain a very high level of admission competitiveness. More to the point, however, is the fact that quality of education is often not directly related to admission standards. Many superior colleges do not have particularly difficult admission requirements.

Myth #6: "Cost is really important in determining where I can go to college, so I will likely have to attend a local school."

Again, not necessarily. Billions of dollars are given to students and families annually to help defray—or in some cases completely pay for—a college education. The federal government, states, individual colleges, and thousands of public and private organizations make funds available to college students. Again, it's just a matter of finding them. Investigate colleges carefully, and use the resources mentioned at the end of the book to help you and your family search for either lower priced colleges or those where you're likely to receive money to help lower the cost of your education. Don't give up before you've even begun! *Chapter 4* provides valuable information about meeting college costs.

Myth #7: "Big colleges are best if you haven't decided on a major."

It's easy to see why this assumption seems true. Because large-size colleges offer more classes, you are more likely to have a wider course selection if you change your field of study or are interested in an unusual major. However, for the many students who need help in choosing a major and or a career, what matters most is not the number of courses but the availability of academic and vocational advice on campus. That means being at a school where teachers and advisors are accessible. At smaller colleges, the faculty has a closer relationship with students. Professors and instructors actively engage with students in discussions about career paths and new fields of study. Although professors at all-size colleges care about their students, it's challenging to get to know a particular student if you see upwards of a thousand students per day! And there's another factor to consider: changing majors (or schools of study within a big university) is more difficult at larger institutions.

Myth #8: "There is only one perfect college for me."

"Perfect" colleges and "dream schools" don't exist. All colleges have good and bad points, and all vary in terms of the attractiveness for any individual student. Your goal is not to find the perfect college; your goal is to research and discover several colleges that best meet your needs.

Myth #9: "I'm a failure if I don't get into College X."

Sometimes students believe that denial at College X or Y or Z means the end of life as they know it, and it can be hard to convince them otherwise. There are countless reasons why students are not accepted at a particular college. Your academic record may not be as strong as that of other applicants. Or College X may be looking for a particular set of traits and—through no fault of your own—you do not have those particular traits. The college may be seeking tuba players or a student from a rural background, and you happen to play the violin and be from the city. Whatever the reasons for your denial from College X, they have no bearing on your future. Your success in college has more to do with attending a school where you can use your talents, be challenged in class, and have a successful experience. If you plan well, you will have several such schools to choose from.

Myth #10: "Some secret strategy can get me admitted to college."

No way. No strategy—secret or open—automatically unlocks the admission door, and you should disregard any source that suggests otherwise. Students who seek letters of recommendation from a Senator or the head of a major corporation (who typically don't know the student) or join clubs in which they have no real interest are trying to strategize. They may agonize for days over an application essay without realizing it's not the topic that matters, as long as you answer the question. Be yourself as you seek admittance to college. Avoid gimmicks, and don't "package" yourself in trappings that aren't you. Trying to gain admission through strategic maneuvering or Machiavellian plotting can backfire badly. College admission officers quickly see through these misplaced energies. Choose colleges that fit, not colleges where you feel your fate depends on complex application strategies.

Myth #11: "Relying on magazine lists of 'Best Colleges' is the best way to determine whether a college is right for me."

Sometimes students are so desperate for information and unsure as to how to start researching colleges that they give great weight to college rankings in magazines and newspapers. But colleges are multifaceted enterprises, and the qualities that make a college right for you may not be assessed in these rankings. No ranking considers the "feel" of a college or what its students are like. No ranking considers every academic field. No ranking measures student engagement in or outside of the classroom. Before you read any list, look carefully at its criteria. Consider whether factors used in the ranking system actually are important to you. And rather than rely too much on rankings, look to the people who know you and the resources described in **Chapter 5** to find the "best" colleges for you.

Myth #12: "I don't know what career I'll pursue, so there's no way I can choose a college."

The fact is, there is only one chance in ten that a person will be doing anything connected with his/her major ten years out of college. If you know what you are likely to major in, fine, that may help to narrow your choices. But if you haven't decided on a career, that's okay too. Think of what else you want in a college: what type of academic experience? what type of social experience? what are the kids like at your ideal college? These and other questions will be discussed in **Chapter 3**. College choice, after all, is not only about life after college. It's also about life during college. Find a place where you will be happy. Meanwhile, high school is a perfect time to consider many career possibilities and research the vast universe of vocational options.

Myth #13: "A good college is hard to get into."

Again, there are hundreds of "good" colleges. In fact, the more I have traveled to colleges, the more fine colleges I have found. What is true is that a brand-name college is often hard to get into whereas a "good match" college is often easy to get into.

Beginning to Dream

Start the college selection process by opening yourself to the excitement and opportunities ahead. Explore colleges in an atmosphere unblocked by preconceptions or myths.

Dream of the future—your success in college and your success in life. Shake off any negativism that may hold you back: "I haven't done that well in high school," "I'm not going to have many college choices," "My test scores are going to prevent my getting into college," "I'm not as good a student as my sister," "I'm never going to live up to my parents' expectations." Focus instead on the possibilities you will have by carefully examining yourself and your goals and by thoroughly exploring college options that are right for you. This attitude will lead to success not only in choosing a college, but also in meeting your other lifetime aspirations.

The college experience will require you to exercise your whole being. You will be called on to think critically and creatively, to be original, to make relationships among new ideas and concepts. Dream of what you can become academically and about the personal and professional value of your new learning and insights. But college is more than just academics; it's the time for growth in other areas. Dream of cultivating leadership skills, enhancing communication skills, and developing a greater sense of others and yourself. Dream of acquiring practical skills like living on a budget, managing time, and lessening stress. Dream about career options so you will feel better about your ultimate career choice. These dreams are the foundation of a successful college experience!

Your first step in transferring your dreams of a successful college experience into reality is picking a college that possesses the right combination of ingredients. The next chapter is designed to start you on that road. Choosing a college will take work, thought, and contemplation. But it will be an important lesson in decision-making and reality testing. The right college is where your dreams can begin to unfold.

Chapter 2
Knowing Yourself

Yes, you start the process of choosing a college with a careful look at yourself, not with a list of colleges. After all, it is your own assessment of your interests, your attitudes, and your abilities that is central to finding a college. Why? Because the purpose of college hunting is to find the right match between you and your eventual college choice. Many students want to start their search by looking at specific colleges. This sounds good, but it is a faulty strategy. Before you start poring over websites, guidebooks, or social media posts, you want to examine yourself as a person and as a student. Such an appraisal will yield data about yourself that will allow you to move with confidence and greater knowledge to the next stages of finding a college.

Worksheets 1 Through 4

The four worksheets in this chapter are essential beginning to your search. **Worksheet 1— Self-Survey for the College Bound**—features 54 items designed to assess self-awareness, which ultimately will help you select the colleges to which you will apply. Complete **Worksheet 1** when you are not rushed and can take a few minutes to think about each statement.

When you finish the Self-Survey, you should score it, and then complete **Worksheet 2—What Your Scores Tell You about Choosing a College.** While the scoring is easy, interpreting your score will take more time but be worth the effort because it will help you make connections between your responses on the Self-Survey and your potential college choices.

Next, complete **Worksheet 3—Activities/Experiences Record.** Here you list significant involvements inside and outside of school. The prompts and questions should help you remember your activities and accomplishments, and the completed list will come in handy as you start preparing your college applications. Be sure to list anything and everything you have done after the eighth grade.

Finally, move to **Worksheet 4—Your Admission/Readiness Profile.** As you complete this worksheet, you'll get a sense of your strengths as a college applicant so that you can realistically assess how you compare with other candidates for admission.

Worksheet 1—Self-Survey for the College-Bound

Respond carefully to these questions about your educational attitudes, goals, and perspectives. Be absolutely truthful and genuine as you answer each question. Keep in mind, there are no "correct" responses. For each item, check the appropriate answer category—"strongly agree," "agree," "lean toward disagree," or "disagree." Even if you are unsure of an answer or your response falls between two categories, answer every question but check only one answer per question.

Item	Strongly Agree	Agree	Lean Toward Disagree	Disagree
1. It takes a whole lot of effort to achieve important goals.	✓			
2. My parents don't have to remind me to study or do my homework.				
3. I usually manage to complete everything on my daily "to-do" list.				

Item	Strongly Agree	Agree	Lean Toward Disagree	Disagree
4. School is fun.	✓			
5. I want to organize myself so I have time for both homework and for out-of-class activities.				
6. I let others know ahead of time when I have a really busy day and can't be disturbed.				
7. I normally am enthused about the classes I am taking.	✓			
8. I'm excited for my college years to begin.				
9. There is more to college than going to class and doing homework.				
10. Once I set a goal, I rarely choose to pursue a different one.				
11. Hard work will lead me to achieving my goals.	✓			
12. I can truly say I enjoy school.	✓			
13. My friends often tell me I'm an empathetic person.	✓			
14. I like work that I'll learn from even if I make a lot of mistakes.	✓			
15. I usually tackle tasks in order of importance.				
16. Once I have a certain idea or project, I don't lose interest.				
17. I am willing to study hard in college, but I also want time to be involved in activities.				
18. On most days, I look forward to going to school.				
19. I often participate in class discussions.				
20. Even for projects that take a few months to complete, I'm usually able to maintain my focus.				
21. Going to college means growing, learning, changing. In other words, it is not just "the thing to do."				
22. I often create schedules for all the tasks I need to complete.				
23. If I don't understand something in class, I typically feel comfortable asking my teacher a question.				
24. I am often asked to mediate if my friends have had an argument.				
25. I finish whatever I begin.				
26. I can usually estimate how much time it is going to take me to complete a specific task.				
27. I'm the type of person who forgives and forgets.				

Item	Strongly Agree	Agree	Lean Toward Disagree	Disagree
28. On most homework assignments, I do everything that needs to be done.				
29. When I'm in college, making friends will be just as important as studying.				
30. I'm usually good at prioritizing my time to get my studying done.				
31. I usually find class discussions stimulating and interesting.				
32. I recognize my emotions as I experience them.				
33. I see many benefits in going to college.				
34. When something is hard, it just makes me want to work more on it, not less.				
35. I want to go to college as much as my parents want me to go.				
36. When I know the answer to a question in class, I usually raise my hand.				
37. My note-taking skills are good.				
38. It is easy for me to identify my favorite class in school.	✓			
39. Setbacks don't discourage me.	✓			
40. Among the aspects that excite me about college are the social connections I'll make.				
41. I use a calendar (paper or electronic) to keep track of the things I need to do.				
42. I appreciate when people, parents, coaches or teachers give me feedback about my performance.				
43. I know my strengths and weaknesses.				
44. I believe I know how to motivate myself to be successful in school.				
45. I can explain why I want to go to college.				
46. When I walk into class, I feel prepared and ready to share what I know.				
47. I am diligent.				
48. I love learning for the sake of learning.	✓			
49. People who are good at a particular skill have spent a lot of time practicing that skill, regardless of natural ability.				
50. I see myself spending lots of time in extracurricular activities while in college.				

Item	Strongly Agree	Agree	Lean Toward Disagree	Disagree
51. I am ready to begin thinking about my future and planning for college.				
52. When I listen to a class lecture, I often make note of the questions I have.				
53. I seldom struggle to build rapport with others.				
54. I rarely do things at the last minute.				

Worksheet 1—Self-Survey Scoring

Now score your Self-Survey

Scoring your answers is easy if you follow these steps:

1. Go back to the first page of your Self-Survey.

   Above the words "Strongly Agree" write a 9.

   Above the words "Agree" write a 6.

   Above the words "Lean Toward Disagree" write a 3.

   Above the words "Disagree" write a 0.

2. Each of the questions you answered corresponds to one of nine overall categories relating to you as a person or as a potential college student. In the categories listed below, the numbers refer to each numbered survey statement.

   For each statement, you will refer back to the survey to see which column you checked.

   Depending on your response—"Strongly Agree," "Agree," "Lean Toward Disagree," or "Disagree"—you enter that number—9, 6, 3, or 0, respectively. For example, starting with the category "Academic Ownership," if you disagreed with the statement "My parents don't have to remind me to study or do my homework," you would enter a "0" on the line next to the number "2."

   Go through and fill in all of the blanks for each of the eight categories.

3. Total your score in each category.

Academic Ownership	**Growth Mindset**	**School Enthusiasm**
2 _____	1 _____	4 _____
28 _____	11 _____	7 _____
30 _____	14 _____	12 _____
37 _____	34 _____	18 _____
44 _____	42 _____	38 _____
54 _____	49 _____	48 _____
Total _____	**Total** _____	**Total** _____

Tenacity	**Participant Learner**	**Academic/Social Balance**
10 _____	19 _____	5 _____
16 _____	23 _____	9 _____
20 _____	31 _____	17 _____
25 _____	36 _____	29 _____
39 _____	46 _____	40 _____
47 _____	52 _____	50 _____
Total _____	**Total** _____	**Total** _____

Emotional Vocabulary	**Eagerness for College**	**Time Management**
13 _____	8 _____	3 _____
24 _____	21 _____	6 _____
27 _____	33 _____	15 _____
32 _____	35 _____	22 _____
43 _____	45 _____	26 _____
53 _____	51 _____	41 _____
Total _____	**Total** _____	**Total** _____

Interpreting Your Self-Survey Scores

The survey you just completed and the interpretation that follows in the next worksheet are intended to encourage you to think about yourself as a college student. By looking at your scores and seeing what they mean within each category, you should glean insight about yourself—your attitudes, strengths and weaknesses, aspirations, and fears. This information will be essential to your college planning process.

The following section provides a description of each category. There is no definitive answer to what a specific score in a category means for you. You will see words like "scores in the mid 30's or higher suggest . . . " and "lower scores suggest . . . " This lack of specificity is purposeful because these scores can be evaluated in many ways. It is up to you to read the descriptions and to determine what, if any, meaning a particular score has for you. Your score in one category might give you insight into something important, and your score in another category might be less meaningful.

Finding meaning in high scores is a bit easier than doing so for lower scores, but remember, there is no hard-and-fast interpretation of a lower score. In the category School Enthusiasm, for example, the first paragraph interprets scores "in the mid 30's or above." The next paragraph is an analysis of the meaning of "lower scores," i.e., a score from 0 to the mid 30's.

Keep in mind that your score—whether higher or lower—is on a continuum. Thus, your interpretation of what your score means in this area will vary if your score was a single digit or in the teens versus the high 20's or low 30's. In other words, the description associated with a low score might be more true of you if your score was a 6 as compared with a 29.

Finally, don't get hung up on the numerical aspects of the interpretation of your scores. The goal here is to provide information that can serve as a springboard in your quest to find colleges that are a good match for you. "High" and "low" numbers are less significant than using the information here to come up with match colleges that correspond with your attributes and beliefs.

Now lets describe each of the categories.

What Do the Categories Mean?

Academic Ownership

If your score in this category is in the mid 30's or higher, you are probably very conscientious when it comes to school. You do your homework without being told, and you make sure you complete your assignments thoroughly. You likely view your learning as your own responsibility, which means you create systems and habits for yourself to succeed academically.

When you receive a grade that's lower than what you hoped for, your first thought is probably not to blame someone else; instead, you may reflect on what you could have done differently and try to learn from your mistakes. In college, you can exercise your natural sense of autonomy by staying organized and trying out new systems and habits that fit your new academic environment.

If your scores are lower, you might find that seeking accountability from others helps keep you focused. When in college, you could try starting study groups with your classmates to make sure you keep track of deadlines and stay on top of everything. Colleges also offer lots of resources—study skills workshops, mentorship programs, and first-year seminars—designed to help new students grow in this area. As you begin to take more ownership over your education, you'll probably notice an increase in self-esteem, too.

Tenacity

Scores in the mid 30's or higher mean that you probably have a considerable amount of grit. Grit includes two things: maintaining your interest in something over a long time (consistency of interest) and sticking with something even when it gets challenging (perseverance of effort). These attributes show that you are tenacious and won't quit when things get tough or when you get bored. You can see projects through until they're finished, which is a valuable quality in college, given that earning a degree is your long-term goal.

Lower scores point to a few possibilities to consider. Perhaps you can persist through difficult tasks, but you get bored quickly, and you find that your interests change frequently. If you feel this describes you, be sure to choose classes in your first year of college that could count toward many different possible majors; an academic advisor can help you choose the best courses. Additionally, attending a college that offers a wide variety of options in the humanities, social sciences, and sciences may be a good strategy for keeping you interested.

Lower scores could also indicate that you maintain your interests over long periods but get discouraged when you're faced with an arduous task. You may find it scary to attempt something at which you're not guaranteed success. If you feel this describes you, college is a great time to start practicing mental tenacity by not giving up and by being kind to yourself when you're not good at something the first time you try it. You may find that perseverance through adversity gets easier with practice when you consistently put effort into something.

Emotional Vocabulary

If you scored in the mid 30's or above in this category, you are probably fluent in the language of emotions and feelings. This means two things: you likely have a high level of empathy for others, and you are probably good at recognizing and regulating your own emotions. Having compassion for others means you can put yourself in others' shoes and view the world from multiple perspectives – even perspectives that may differ from your own. College will present you with different viewpoints, and having empathy will allow you to analyze arguments from many different angles. Your empathy and your ability to recognize and regulate your emotions will also serve you well as you adjust to an entirely new environment, which is bound to be stressful at times.

Lower scores may indicate that you struggle to relate to the experiences of others or to your own emotions. Maybe you've lived in the same place and interacted with the same group of people your entire life and find it hard to understand the experiences of others you don't yet know. This is very common; building one's emotional vocabulary is a skill that is developed over time and life experience. Expanding your emotional vocabulary will help you not only connect with others during college as you develop new and meaningful friendships but also take care of yourself during stressful times. One way to grow in your ability to recognize and regulate your emotions is to practice mindfulness, patience, and forgiveness of yourself and others.

Growth Mindset

Scores in the mid 30's and higher show that you believe hard work is necessary to achieve your goals. In other words, you are aware that raw talent is not enough to achieve excellence; mastery of a skill or knowledge also requires dedication and effort. Knowing this, you believe you can get better at things provided you keep trying. If you fail at something the first time you try it, you aren't overly concerned; you see initial failure as an opportunity to learn and grow.

Lower scores in this category could indicate that you have more of a fixed mindset. You may believe that you're either good at something or you're not, which could lead you to give up on activities or projects if you don't experience immediate success. When you were growing up, you may have shown natural talent in certain areas. Perhaps you came to believe that your natural talent was more important to your success than your practice and dedication. However, this way of approaching life can lead to a tendency to give up too quickly on new endeavors. College will undoubtedly present you with new challenges. Now's the time to start shifting your mindset by permitting yourself to fail and viewing complex academic challenges as conquerable through hard work and dedication.

Participant Learner

If your score in this category is in the mid 30's or higher, you probably take an active rather than passive approach to learning. You are not comfortable merely taking notes and regurgitating the teacher's lectures—you want to get involved! You usually do the homework your teachers assign, not because you have to, but because it helps you learn. You participate in class discussion, enjoy it, and learn from your peers. You study the textbooks and may read additional material on a topic that interests you. Because learning and understanding are so important to you, you are assertive in asking teachers and fellow students questions. You likely will be most comfortable at colleges where professors are readily available, and lecture classes are not huge. In addition, you will want opportunities for discussions and seminars as part of your college experience. High scorers should consider smaller colleges.

Lower scorers in this category have several factors to consider. You may be interested in and committed to learning but prefer to learn quietly and deliberately rather than participate verbally in class. Course lectures, reading, and out-of-class assignments are ordinarily sufficient for you to understand the material. For you, class size probably will not be as significant a factor. Lower scores suggest that you may not mind being in a large class, and a bigger university would meet your needs.

Eagerness for College

Scores in the mid to high 30's or above signal that you anticipate college in a favorable way and are looking forward to the collegiate experience. Your adjustment to college will likely be easy because your enthusiasm will prove a great asset in learning to master collegiate life. Although you may have some concerns about college, your attitude is generally positive. Because you played a primary role in deciding to attend college, you may already have specific goals to make the most of your college years.

Lower scores can be interpreted in several ways. Just because you scored low here doesn't mean that you are not "college material" or are dreading the college experience. Eagerness for college tends to ebb and flow during the high school years. A lower score is worth thinking about, however. Are you motivated to attend college? You will want to give special consideration to how you can make college a satisfying and productive experience. Some fears about college—such as leaving home and being independent—are perfectly normal. If your score was lower in this category, involving yourself in the planning and decision-making processes will help you feel more in control and less like you are being pushed into college. However, if you continue to feel some apathy as college draws near, you may want to think carefully about and seek assistance with the timing and the nature of your college years. You might want to consider options like work, an apprenticeship, trade school, volunteering, military, AmeriCorps, Peace Corps, travel, or learning from home (via online courses).

School Enthusiasm

If you scored in the mid 30's or higher, you probably feel comfortable with the tasks and central qualities of school. In general, you like attending classes and have positive feelings about the academic nature of school.

If your score is lower here, there are several possible interpretations. You may enjoy some of the social features of school more than the actual classes, teachers, and classroom information. You may not have found school to be a successful academic experience, and your struggle with school has affected your attitude toward it. Your school attitude may impact your feelings about planning for college, your willingness to enter a challenging college environment, the level of competitiveness you prefer, as well as your motivation to stay in school. Do you have the motivation to be successful in college? You may not have enjoyed high school because particular characteristics of your school may not have been suitable for you. If that is the case, you have a chance to choose the college that provides the kind of environment that suits you. Your analysis of the factors that matter to you in a college will be fundamental in finding a college you can be excited about attending. You also may want to consider these questions: Is the time right to enter college? Would you benefit from a year of travel, work, or some other activity before entering college?

Academic/Social Balance

If you scored in the mid to high 30's and above, both academics and extracurricular experiences are priorities for you. You will want to choose a college where you can have a balanced life—where you can pursue your studies, participate in sports or other activities, and still have some time for yourself. Colleges known for a "work hard/play hard" philosophy may appeal to you, but consider your college choices carefully; it's easy to take that philosophy too much to heart and end up burning out or getting in over your head.

You will want to choose a college where you are academically similar to the majority of students, where you are as likely as anyone else to understand the material in your classes, where you can spend about the same amount of time studying and still have a life outside of the classroom. In researching colleges, look carefully at the characteristics of students who enroll. What were their grade point averages? Test scores? Did they take courses in high school fairly similar to the ones you have chosen?

A lower score in this category indicates a lack of balance between academics and social activities. Perhaps you are keenly focused on academics and want college to be all about learning. If academics are your highest or even your only priority, you may be comfortable at a college that is academically intense. Alternatively, your score may indicate you value your social life more than your studies and want college to be all about having fun. If social experiences matter most, you will want to consider colleges where the academics are not so rigorous that you wouldn't have time to get involved in campus activities and socialize with friends.

Time Management

Scores in the mid to high 30's and above indicate that you likely are very good at managing your time to complete all your tasks. You create "to-do" lists and schedules to ensure you stay on top of everything, and because you're able to estimate how long various tasks take you, you probably make sure you have time available before you commit to something new. Given that you will have more autonomy over your time in college, you are likely to continue to hone your time management skills.

Lower scores in this category suggest that managing your time can be challenging for you. Maybe you wait until the last minute to complete assignments or study for exams.

Or perhaps you rely on others—your teachers or your parents—to keep you on track or remind you of upcoming deadlines.

Throughout the college application process and when you're in college, managing your time effectively will be an essential skill. Strategies that can help you improve in this area and ensure you accomplish important tasks on time include keeping a calendar, setting deadlines for yourself, and using a daily planner to check off items as you complete them.

Worksheet 2—What Your Scores Tell You about Choosing a College

You've now scored each of the categories and read about what your scores mean. Look back on the categories where your scores are highest and lowest. Keep in mind that a self-survey such as this one, relying on numerical results, is inherently flawed. The self-survey is only meaningful if you use it to think about the issues presented in the categories and, incorporating the self-knowledge gleaned from your scores, build your college list in a productive, informed way.

The following questions pertaining to your scores encourage you to analyze, clarify, and understand what your scores mean in the context of choosing your college.

1. *List below the three categories in which you received the highest scores:*

   Highest score category _____

   Second highest score category _____

   Third highest score category _____

2. *In your own words, describe what your highest score category says about you and your college-going needs.*

   _____

   _____

   _____

   _____

   _____

   _____

3. *In your own words, describe what your second highest score category says about you and your college-going needs.*

    _____

    _____

    _____

    _____

    _____

    _____

4. *List below the two categories in which you received the lowest scores:*

    Lowest score category _____

    Second lowest score category _____

5. *In your own words, describe what your lowest score category says about you and your college-going needs.*

    _____

    _____

    _____

    _____

    _____

    _____

6. *Look at your score in the categories "Tenacity" and "Growth Mindset." What does your score indicate about staying with tasks even when the going gets tough? How do you assess your motivation for college success?*

    _____

    _____

    _____

    _____

    _____

    _____

7. **Look at your score in the category "Participant Learner." What does it indicate in terms of size of the college that is right for you? Which is better—smaller classes or larger classes?**

_____

_____

_____

_____

_____

_____

8. **Look at all of your scores. What have you learned about yourself that might be helpful in assessing your strengths and weaknesses as a potential college student? Did you learn anything else about yourself that may help you in "fitting in" at a college, academically and socially?**

_____

_____

_____

_____

_____

_____

Worksheet 3—Activities/Experiences Record

I. **List your in-school and out-of-school activities. Examples: student government, drama, publications, sports, clubs. List them in order of their importance to you. (Use additional sheets if necessary.)**

Name of Activity	School Years Involved				Hours /Week	Hours /Year	Positions Held
	9	10	11	12			

II. **Creative work, hobbies, interests or anything else not listed above to which you have devoted substantial time.**

_____

_____

_____

_____

_____

_____

III. **Travel. Describe where you have traveled in the last three years.**

_____
_____
_____
_____
_____
_____
_____

IV. **Academic honors. Describe any scholastic distinctions or honors you have won in grades 9-12. List the grade level for each. Examples: Honor Roll—11, 12; Certificate in French—10.**

_____
_____
_____
_____
_____
_____
_____

V. **Other honors or distinctions (athletic, literary, musical, artistic, or other).**

_____
_____
_____
_____
_____
_____

VI. Employment

Nature of Work (clerk, delivery, etc.)	Employer (Name of Company)	Dates of Employment	Approximate Weekly Hours

VII. How have you spent the last two summers?

Last summer:

_____

_____

_____

_____

_____

_____

Previous summer:

_____

_____

_____

_____

_____

_____

Worksheet 4—Your Admission/Readiness Profile

This worksheet helps you assess your strengths as a college applicant. Although it provides insights for all students, it may be most valuable for students considering colleges with very selective admissions. The worksheet lists the attributes and accomplishments that admission committees take particular note of as they review applications. Completing this worksheet should give you a sense of how you might compare with other applicants. Some questions are factual and others are subjective. Your straightforward responses and your best judgment will allow you to evaluate yourself realistically as a candidate for admission.

In sections I through VII of this worksheet, the preparation that is considered the strongest and most attractive (to the colleges) is marked with ①, the next strongest is marked with ②, and the next strongest with ③. Please keep in mind that most colleges in the United States are relatively easy to get into. Even students who are ③'s on this scale have plenty of good colleges from which to choose.

I. **Coursework. For each subject listed, check the number of years of coursework (grades 9–12) you will have completed upon graduation. In other words, mark the number of years of study in each subject that you expect to have completed over four years of high school by making one check per subject.**

  A. English
  _____✓_____ 4 years (includes at least 2 in writing) ①
  _____ 3 plus years ②
  _____ Less than 3 years ③

  B. Mathematics (algebra, geometry, trigonometry, math analysis, pre-calculus, calculus)
  _____✓_____ 4 years ①
  _____ 3 plus years ②
  _____ 2 plus years ②
  _____ Less than 2 years ③

  C. Foreign Language (remember, for grades 9 through 12 only)
  _____✓_____ 4 years ①
  _____ 3 plus years ①
  _____ 2 plus years ②
  _____ 1 plus year ③
  _____ Less than 1 year ③

D. Social Studies (history, government, psychology, etc.)

_____✓_____ 4 years ①

_____ 3 plus years ②

_____ 2 plus years ②

_____ Less than 2 years ③

E. Science

_____✓_____ 4 years (includes many lab courses) ①

_____ 4 years (includes few lab courses) ②

_____ 3 plus years ②

_____ 2 plus years ②

_____ Less than 2 years ③

F. Have you taken at least a year of art, music, or theater?

_____✓_____ Yes ①

_____ No ②

II. *Class Rank. Check where you rank in relation to the other students in your graduating class. If your school does not rank students, make an educated guess.*

_____ Top 3% ①

_____ Top 10% ①   idk

_____ Top 33% ②

_____ Top 50% ②

_____ Lower 50% ③

III. *Test scores to date. Check appropriate columns for tests you have taken.**

SAT Evidence Based Reading and Writing

_____ 710 or above

_____ 660-700

_____ 590-650   not yet

_____ 510-580

_____ 500 or below

ACT Composite

_____ 31 or above

_____ 28-30

_____ 25-27

_____ 21-24

_____ 20 or below

SAT Mathematics

_____ 710 or above

_____ 660-700

_____ 590-650

_____ 510-580

_____ 500 or below

*Submission of test scores is optional at many colleges.

IV. Extracurricular Activities. Review your completed Worksheet 3, Activities/ Experiences Record. Check the statement that best describes the extent of your involvements.

_____Extensive record of involvement in activities and/or individual talent of an extraordinary nature. Recognition extends beyond the local school or community and/or perceived as one of the most outstanding persons in the school or the community. ①

_____ Intensive leadership demonstrated in a major school or community activity (editor-in-chief of newspaper, president of student council, etc.) and/or individual talent recognized as superior. Substantial recognition for achievements. ①

_____ Significant leadership position or major participant in school or community activities and/or one or two very fine individual talents. Appropriate recognition for achievements. ②

_____ Some leadership positions or memberships in several clubs or community activities or a significant individual talent. ②

_____ Few in- or out-of-school involvements. ③

V. Basic Academic Skills. In assessing these basic tools, think about the following areas:

- Your note-taking ability.
- Your ability to read with speed and comprehension.
- Your ability to write with clarity and substance.
- Your ability to research.

You may feel better about one of these skills, not so satisfied about another. But in your best judgment, and compared with other students, check the one item below that seems most true of your basic academic tools.

_____ Excellent in basic academic skills. ①

_____ Good in basic academic skills. ②

_____ Average in basic academic skills. ②

_____ Below-average in basic academic skills. ③

VI. Study Skills and Time Management. In assessing these qualities, think about the following.

- Your ability to complete assignments on time.
- Your ability to set and meet deadlines for papers, for review of class material, and so on.
- Your ability to handle pressure.
- Your ability to focus on what needs to be done.

While you may be better in one area and weaker in another, check the one item below that seems most true of you.

_____ Excellent in study skills and time management. ①

_____ Good in study skills and time management. ②

_____ Average in study skills and time management. ②

_____ Below-average in study skills and time management. ③

VII. Academic Recommendations. Check the one set of words and phrases most likely to appear in your teacher recommendations:

_____ "best student I've ever taught," "unbelievably curious," "a real scholar," "here are specific examples of academic/intellectual depth . . ." ①

_____ "one of my best students in class," "loves learning," "sees relationships between concepts that other students miss . . ." ①

_____ "a good deal of intellectual potential," "tries awfully hard," "I see evidence of academic prowess." ②

_____ "personally, he/she is a good kid," "likable," "completes work on time," "an above-average student," "lots of potential for growth." [recommendations that tend toward description of personal—rather than academic— qualities] ③

VIII. Rank Ordering of Admission Strengths. Rank each of the following qualities as they apply to you as a college applicant. For example, if you feel your "test scores" are your strongest feature as viewed by colleges, mark that item with a one (1).

_____ Coursework (strong, competitive courses)

_____ Grades

_____ Academic recommendations

_____ Rank in class

_____ Extracurricular activities

_____ Test scores (if submitted)

_____ Personal attributes/personality

_____ Work experiences

_____ Other (specify) _____

IX. Summarize Your Admission Profile. Look at your responses to items I through VIII. Comment on your strengths and weaknesses as a college applicant. In how many areas (I–VIII), do you show the very strongest preparation (strongest is indicated with ①)? What about weaker areas? Can you do anything now to strengthen your preparation?

_____

_____

_____

_____

_____

_____

Evaluate Your Admission Profile

What have you learned about yourself as a candidate for admission? How do you assess your readiness for college? What strengths about yourself will you want to emphasize in the admission process? What weaknesses will you need to take into consideration?

Next, share your responses on *Worksheets 2* and *4* with your parents, your college counselor, and/or a good friend. How do they react? Do they have any additions or comments about any of your answers? Make notes of their comments and additions on the worksheets. Your counselor will help you analyze what your responses to these worksheets say about your college choices. Regularly update *Worksheet 3* with any new activities, work experiences, or awards.

Sometimes learning about yourself can be painful because your sense of yourself may not be what you wish it were or hope it will become. You may have found you are not as strong a college applicant as you thought you were. But keep in mind the essential message of *Chapter 1*: there are many colleges from which to choose, and your happiness and your comfort in the right educational environment is what is most important. In life, each of us deals with the reality of our situation and with the knowledge of our strengths and weaknesses.

As you progress through the admission process, keep your strengths in mind but also let your weaknesses point toward ways you can improve. It is not what you are today that is the most important—it is what you will become after your undergraduate years that will be most meaningful to a fulfilling professional career and a happy life.

Using the knowledge you have gained about yourself in this chapter, you should now be able to identify the qualities that will make a college a good match for you. That is the purpose of *Chapter 3*.

Chapter 3

What Are You Looking For In a College?

Of all the chapters in the book, this one is perhaps the most important. Here, you will discover those qualities or characteristics that make a particular college a good fit or match for you. *Chapter 2* was about you. It allowed you to assess yourself on a number of traits that are pertinent to your college planning. Now, armed with that information, you are asked to learn about some of the characteristics of colleges that make them special. Once you have named and identified your preferences, you will be able to move on to the chapter on costs (*Chapter 4*), and then, in *Chapter 5*, you will list colleges that are right for you.

When you finish this chapter, you will have an answer to the question: What am I looking for in a college? After reading this chapter, you will have considered a number of qualities found in colleges and universities: size, location, admission difficulty, academic offerings, and so forth. Each is explained in terms of how it might affect your college experience. So, as you read about each characteristic, think about yourself and your preferences. If, for example, you still have trouble identifying your own preferences for size of college after reading about that characteristic, then stop and reflect on yourself and your school experiences so far. What is the size of your high school? Have you felt comfortable there? Have you ever attended a smaller or larger school? How did that feel?

The key to using this chapter effectively is to answer the questions honestly and thoroughly. Try not to anticipate how your parents or friends would want you to respond. Answer for yourself. Students usually know what they prefer and where they will do well.

Maybe you are wondering why various college qualities are even important since you simply want the "best" school you can get into. But in the context of college, "best" means what is ideal for you, not what is "best" in some generic sense. The right approach to finding a college is to identify the characteristics that fit you and will make for four successful, happy, and productive years. Yes, it will be time-consuming to think about the qualities colleges offer, but such an analysis yields better college options. Regardless of the college you select, you will know why you chose that particular school, and knowing why you have made a choice is perhaps one of the most important skills you can develop.

As you progress through this chapter, remember there are no easy answers or correct responses to questions about the right size college for you, the right location, or the right academic environment. You may be the kind of person who finds success in a range of college sizes, locations, and academic environments. On the other hand, in some environments you might thrive as a student, but in others, you could find barriers to your success. Completing *Worksheet 5* will help you build your ideal college profile. Pinpointing these qualities, in turn, will lead you to a list of colleges that are right for you. Remember also that this is the beginning of your college search. What you seek in a college may change over the months. This worksheet starts the process of thinking and learning about characteristics that distinguish one college from the next.

Allow an hour or so to work your way methodically through the worksheet. First, read the description of each quality carefully. Then think about how that quality relates to you as a person and as a potential college student. Finally, complete the questions asked of you about each quality.

After you have finished *Worksheet 5*, proceed to *Worksheet 6*—a summary of the characteristics you are looking for in a college. Completing it will give you an overview of college features that will lead to your academic and social success.

Worksheet 5—Qualities That Will Make a College Right for You

When you see numbers from 1 to 5 sandwiched between two statements, circle the number that best reflects your level of preference. Circle 1 if you have a strong preference for the quality listed on the left. Circle 5 if you have a strong preference for the quality listed on the right. Use 2, 3, or 4 to reflect varying levels of preference.

Quality 1—Size

Colleges vary in size from under 100 to more than 60,000 students. As you think about this quality, try to picture the size college that is best for you academically AND socially. The following considerations may help you.

Smaller colleges. Smaller colleges provide students with many benefits. First, they can be just as diverse, fun, and interesting as larger schools. Students at these schools often rave about the range of opportunities and the depth of their friendships.

Second, because classes are more intimate than those at large universities, they allow for greater interaction between student and professor. You'll have more opportunities to contribute in class, and it's likely you'll really know your professors. By knowing your professors, you can benefit from their expertise and they can help you with any academic weak points. Further, they will be able to write you knowledgeable recommendations for jobs or graduate schools. Smaller colleges are best if you prefer discussion classes (where you are a participant) as opposed to lecture classes (where the teacher does most of the talking). You are also more likely to be able to register for the classes you desire. And at smaller colleges, you experience less competition for the use of academic facilities such as library resources and specialized equipment.

In addition, smaller colleges tend to place greater emphasis on personal development. In other words, it's easier for students to learn about themselves: their interests, abilities, and possible career paths. The best preparation for students who are unsure of their career direction is a liberal arts and sciences curriculum found at most small colleges. A college does not need to offer every one of your potential career majors to be a good place to prepare for your future; many studies have highlighted career successes that began with a liberal arts and sciences education. At smaller colleges, teaching is usually the top priority of faculty members—research may be less important. This emphasis may mean more exciting classroom experiences (which often result in increased understanding and higher grades). At larger universities, in contrast, you may be taught by graduate students, not professors.

Smaller colleges provide greater opportunities to participate in extracurricular activities because you don't have to be a superstar to get involved. If you don't find the club or organization that feeds your particular interest, you can always start one. You might enjoy a smaller college if you want to fairly quickly find a place in a new community. Because it is difficult to get "lost," small colleges often facilitate the development of student confidence. Don't discount the advantages of being a significant fish in a small pond—it can do wonders for your self-esteem and sense of accomplishment.

Larger colleges. Larger colleges also offer many benefits. Here, you'll find great range and variety in the courses offerings. You may be able to explore (and perhaps take classes in) two different fields of study— for example, arts and sciences and engineering. Also, students who are very undecided about the subjects they want to study may feel that large universities (offering many strong majors) are their safest educational choice. In addition, special advanced facilities and equipment are available at many large universities. Students whose learning style is more listening-based may prefer lectures to classes that are more discussion-oriented. Many students may appreciate the anonymity that a large school offers.

At large universities, students invariably find more activities from which to choose. Nationally known and popular sports teams not only increase a school's name recognition but also promote school spirit and camaraderie among students. At colleges with large student populations, there are organizations and clubs that focus on an array of interests and serve all kinds of social groups.

Be cautious about generalizations. Important as they are, size considerations often cause students to limit the field of potential colleges too early in the process of choosing a college. Students who cross all larger colleges off their list before they even begin should be aware that larger colleges may vary in terms of how much personal attention is available from teachers, career advisors, and others. Students who reject smaller colleges as too vanilla or boring should know that small colleges can be just as diverse and just as fun. They're also overlooking the more than 80% of private colleges in the U.S.—and almost a quarter of the nation's public colleges—that have enrollments under 2,500.

Just because you attended a large high school doesn't mean you should attend a large college or that there is something regressive about going to a small college. On the other hand, students from smaller high schools should not assume they are now "ready" for a bigger school. It's also true that students from smaller high schools aren't necessarily happier at a small college. Some students make false assumptions when comparing high school size with college size. The reality is that college is very different from high school, and your consideration of size is dependent on many factors, including the dimensions you see outlined in this worksheet.

High desire for accessible teachers.	1	2	3	4	5	Low desire for accessible teachers.
I would likely get better grades in small classes.	1	2	3	4	5	I would likely get similar grades in small or large classes.
More discussion-oriented classes.	1	2	3	4	5	More lecture-oriented classes.
I learn best discussing ideas and interacting with the instructor and students.	1	2	3	4	5	I learn best by reading, listening, taking notes.
Desire for tutors/ extra assistance.	1	2	3	4	5	No desire for tutors/ extra assistance.
A close-knit, family-like environment.	1	2	3	4	5	A place where I can blend in with the crowd.

First, look at the following size distinctions. (These distinctions are arbitrary and are intended merely to assist you in considering general size parameters.)

Small size—fewer than 3,000 students

Medium size—between 3,000 and 10,000 students

Large size—between 10,000 and 20,000 students

Largest size—more than 20,000 students

Now, on the basis of the discussion and your circled responses above, check those sizes that you feel are best for you.

_____ Small_____ Medium _____ Large _____Largest

Any comments/further thoughts about the size of your ideal college?

_____

_____

_____

Quality 2—Academic Environment

To determine what kind of academic environment will be right for you, you will need to think about the intellectual intensity you are comfortable with and the level of academic pressure that motivates you without making you feel stressed out or frustrated. Naturally, since college is an academic undertaking, classes and other academic concerns make up the bulk of your collegiate experience. Finding the appropriate level of academic challenge is important to your choice of colleges. Think about how much intellectual intensity is right for you. Do you want a college where you must work hard and study hard, or would you prefer one where you could earn respectable grades without knocking yourself out? Think carefully about how much time you want to spend on academic pursuits in college. If you truly enjoy talking about ideas and intellectual subjects, you may choose the "very academic" side of the "Intellectual Intensity" scale that follows.

Also, think here about your response to academic pressure and competition from others. Are you at home with a tremendous workload? Do you prioritize well? Can you discipline yourself? If your answers are "yes," you should select a vigorous academic environment. If, however, you prefer to perform consistently at the top of your class, if you become distraught with a grade lower than an A, or if you don't work well under stress, you may respond better to a college with normal academic pressure.

Intellectual Intensity

Very academic/ scholarly emphasis	1	2	3	4	5	Balance between academic/ social sides of campus life

Academic Pressure

Ready/able to handle the most vigorous academic environment	1	2	3	4	5	Ready/able to handle normal academic pressure

Other Academic/Curricular Qualities

In addition to offering certain concentrated areas of potential study (majors), colleges vary in terms of other academic qualities. Would you enjoy more freedom or more structure insofar as courses you are required to take? Would work experiences, internships, or the availability of independent study enhance your academic success? Would you like a particularly strong study abroad experience? Do you want to prepare for the military? Many academic variables are included on the following list. **Check any that you would like in your college.**

_____ internships/work experiences

_____ learning resources (learning center, tutors, extra time on tests, etc.)

_____ considerable freedom in choosing courses

_____ programs for students with learning style differences (LD, ADD, ADHD, etc.)

_____ independent study options

_____ applying what I learn to real world problems

_____ preparation for the military

_____ more hands-on learning opportunities

_____ counseling/psychological/medical services

_____ courses geared to my specific academic/career interests

_____ excellent study abroad programs

_____ research opportunities

_____ personalized academic advising

_____ personalized career advising

_____ writing center

Is there anything else related to the academic environment that is important to you? If so, describe it here:

_____

_____

_____

Quality 3—Academic Offerings

This category refers to your potential college major and not your potential career. It's important for you to keep that distinction in mind. A major is a subject you enjoy and would like to study in college. Do you enjoy English or history? Does math or communication sound interesting? **Appendix F, Possible Major Fields of Study**, should spark some ideas.

In this section, you are asked to mark where you stand on the continuum between "A liberal arts and sciences college is best" and "A college that will prepare me for a specific career after four years of college is best." Liberal arts and sciences is the term used to describe the most general and most common form of undergraduate education in the U.S. It includes the humanities (English, languages, music, art, philosophy, etc.), the social sciences (psychology, history, political science, etc.), and the "hard" sciences (biology, mathematics, geology, etc.). Many liberal arts and sciences schools also provide coursework in business and engineering. The liberal arts and sciences often serve as a springboard for future study (for example, graduate school, law school, medical school, or business school) and for the world of work.

If you are uncertain about your career, then you should select a liberal arts and sciences curriculum where you can gain a broad education. On the other hand, you may want to take more courses in an area that already interests you. The classes in career-oriented schools will more directly relate to careers in such areas as engineering, business, physical therapy, or architecture on completion of your undergraduate degree.

It is perfectly okay not to know what your ultimate career will be. Most high school students do not know, and many who enter college with a career picked out change their mind (and major) at least once before graduating. In some ways, coming to the wrong conclusion too early about a career is worse than not knowing. Most high school students have not been exposed to many career alternatives, making a final career decision premature. The undergraduate years can be a time of discovery about yourself and your career goals.

A liberal arts and sciences college is best.	1	2	3	4	5	A college that prepares me for a specific career after four years of college is best.
I want a broad-based education so I can consider several careers.	1	2	3	4	5	I would like to focus on classes that are relevant to my current career interests.

If you already feel confident in your selection of a career goal and want a college that offers your particular program, enter the name of your program in the space provided below. If you're still unsure, what subjects would you like to learn more about? And/ or which subjects will you consider as a major? (Some colleges allow you to have more than one major.) Remember, if you need ideas to get you started, refer to the list provided in **Appendix F.**

Possible programs, majors, or subjects of study:

_____

_____

_____

What career(s) have you considered? If none, say so.

_____

_____

_____

Quality 4—Cost/Availability of Financial Aid

Costs vary greatly from one college to another. Many students, however, make too many assumptions about cost too early in the process of choosing a college. There are many forms of financial aid available. Although most aid is given (naturally) to those who can demonstrate need (by the results of a standardized financial aid analysis using forms such as the Free Application for Federal Student Aid), aid is also available for students who have achieved academic excellence or those with special abilities. Most students take out loans to pay for their college education. Talk to your parents and advisors about the pros and cons of accumulating debt.

Perhaps no factor in college selection is as potentially limiting as cost. There are so many myths associated with cost. Students and families may believe that little money is available, that only poverty-stricken families receive aid, or that students need to be super scholars to receive money from colleges. The truth is that enormous resources are available for families who take the time to explore financial aid opportunities. The reference section of this book provides a starting list of places to get information about college costs and financial aid. *Chapter 4* also lists financial aid resources.

On the following continuum, indicate the extent to which cost/availability of aid is a consideration in your choice of a college. It is quite important to talk this over with your family. You might want to read *Chapter 4* (and have your parents do the same) before completing these questions.

Cost is a major factor in choosing a college.	1	2	3	4	5	Cost is a minor factor in choosing a college.
I need to do a thorough search of my financial aid options.	1	2	3	4	5	No search of financial aid options is necessary.
Cost will lead me to an in-state college. . . or one that costs less. . . or one where I can get a scholarship.	1	2	3	4	5	Cost will not lead me in these directions.

Comments about cost/financial aid in your college search:

_____

_____

_____

Quality 5—Religion

The extent of religious influence varies from college to college. Some colleges have very little or no religious influence. Other schools may be related to a particular religious denomination, but are not governed or influenced by the church; these schools also tend to have very little religious influence. There are other colleges—Christian colleges, for example—that have far closer relationships to a denomination that extend to required religion classes and/or religious practices (such as chapel services).

Regardless of the extent of religious life, you might desire a college where many, if not most, of the students belong to your religion. Is this factor important to you in selecting a college?

Religious life is an important factor in choosing a college.	1	2	3	4	5	Religious life is not a factor in choosing in choosing a college.
I want a college where religious life is emphasized.	(1)	2	3	4	5	I do not care about whether religious life is emphasized.
I'd like to be at a college where many students share my religious background.	1	2	3	4	5	Having many students of my religious background is not a significant college planning variable.

Comments about religious influence:

_____
_____
_____

Quality 6—Ethnicity

Latino, Latina, American Indian, Asian, and African-American students may benefit in many ways by attending a college with a high number of students who belong to the same ethnic group. For example, for the African-American student, predominantly Black colleges offer students the opportunity to interact with Black role models, to develop a network of contacts who can be helpful in getting jobs, and to learn in a comfortable environment. Many respected leaders in government, education, and other professions are graduates of these institutions. Similarly, students who might feel isolated on predominantly "white" campuses often benefit from the camaraderie and closeness that comes from being with others who share their heritage.

Would the presence of other students of your heritage foster your sense of belonging? Would you feel like an outsider if you were one of only a few students of your ethnic background? Are you interested in specialized programs for minority students?

It's important that I attend a college where many students share my ethnic/racial heritage.	1	2	3	4	5	It's unimportant that I attend a college where many students share my heritage.

Comments about racial/ethnic issues in my choice of college:

_____
_____
_____

Quality 7—Coeducation or Single Sex

This consideration is predominately for women, although there are some fine all-male colleges as well. Don't be too hasty here. Both women's and men's colleges offer special educational advantages and ought to be carefully considered. For example, several studies have found that students at women's colleges are more academically involved in classes, are more likely to pursue advanced degrees, and show more intellectual self-esteem, compared with their counterparts in coeducational institutions. Furthermore, a women's college offers women more opportunities for academic success in an environment where they don't need to compete with men for both classroom time and positions of campus leadership. Women's colleges are just as fun, just as interesting, and, in many ways, can be just as "real world" as coed schools.

What kind of school would you consider?

_____ Coed_____ Men _____ Women

Quality 8—Student Body Characteristics

Identifying the characteristics about students with whom you will feel most at home can be meaningful as you contemplate your college choices. Think about the traits that you would like to see in your fellow students. What follows is a list of words and phrases that describe people and personalities. *Circle those qualities that describe members of the student body at a college you would like to attend. In the blanks provided, list any other characteristics that you would like to find in your future classmates.*

Keep in mind that most colleges enroll a wide variety of students. This exercise is designed to identify the personality characteristics and values of students at a college that is a good match for you. As you research colleges and as you visit, pay attention to words or phrases used to describe schools of interest to you. See if there are similarities between your words and college descriptions.

adventurous	dress-conscious	(motivated)	spirited
~~aggressive~~ *no thank you*	energetic	(nonjudgmental)	spontaneous
ambitious	entreprenerial	(open)	supportive
artsy	focused	(opinionated)	tightly knit
athletic	(friendly)	(outdoorsy)	tolerant
(balanced)	fun	patient	traditional
career-oriented	(good values)	politically active	unconventional
caring	goofy	practical	understanding
(compassionate)	idealistic	realistic	well-behaved
conservative	independent	respectful	interested in cultural activities
cosmopolitan	(innovative)	risk-taking	(interested in learning for learning's sake) :)
(creative)	involved	scholarly	
disciplined	laid back	sensitive	
(diverse)	liberal	serious	
down-to-earth	moral	social	

Other characteristics you'd like to see in your fellow students:

|
_____
|
_____
|
_____

If you circled more than five qualities, now go back and put a check mark next to the five that are most important to you.

Finally, take a look at the following continuum. Students at the colleges on the left side of the continuum are traditional; in other words, they are like students you'd find on most campuses. Students at the colleges on the right side of the continuum are more alternative, free-spirited, and independent-minded. The distinction here is arbitrary (and involves generalizing), but your response can be helpful in thinking about broad categories of students at your "good-match" college. If you can't decide, or if this variable is unimportant, or if you could fit into either side, circle 3.

A more traditional student body is best for me.	1	2	3	4	5	An alternative, free-spirited, independent-minded student body is best for me.

Comments about the students at your ideal college:

_____

_____

_____

Quality 9—Student Life

Colleges differ from each other in many ways, and many of these differences relate to student life. Your satisfaction with your college choice is likely to depend on how comfortable and content you feel on campus. ***Check any of the following characteristics that are important to you.***

_____ most students live on-campus

_____ lots of spectator sports

_____ an environmentally concerned student body

_____ going to athletic games is a big social event

_____ lots of students participate in intramural sports

_____ fraternities/sororities are available

_____ specialized programs for women/gay/multicultural students

_____ lots of weekend activities

_____ the food is good

✓ a safe campus no duh

✓ a beautiful campus TREES!!!

_____ ramps/easy access to buildings

_____ many leadership opportunities available

_____ nice residence halls/living spaces

_____ where a sense of community exists

_____ where I'm recognized for accomplishments outside of class

_____ where I don't feel like a number

_____ community service/volunteer opportunities

_____ very spirited

What are some other characteristics of student life that will make your college experience a better one?

_____

_____

_____

_____

Quality 10—Activities (Including Athletics)

You may desire a normal variety of activities, or you may be looking for a college that offers some specific activity. You might want to continue a high school activity or you might want to develop new interests. For example, you might want to get involved in clubs that relate to you career or professional interests. Would you like to participate in sports? Which ones? At the varsity, club, or intramural level? Do you want to be a leader and/or develop your leadership skills? Are you looking for theater or art or music involvements? Are there other clubs or organizations that appeal to you in such areas as religion, international students, outdoor/recreation, community service, ethnic/culture, political, or academic? *Appendix G, Potential College Activities List, includes an array of potential college activities. In the space provided below, jot down those that interest you:*

_____

_____

_____

_____

_____

_____

_____

Quality 11—Big Name School or Best Fit School?

Students vary in the priority they place on attending a well-known college or university. Students who are very focused on attending a "name" college or university sometimes put that desire above other factors in choosing a school, and as a result, totally disregard whether the "name" college is a good overall fit for them. On the other hand, students looking for a school that is a good match for them look at all the factors or qualities that a college possesses—its size, programs offered, characteristics of the students, quality of faculty, location, and so forth. It's fine for an "A" student to want to attend an excellent quality college. But remember that dozens and dozens of colleges have superior professors, outstanding academic facilities, and a high percentage of graduates admitted to top graduate schools. Most colleges have excellent networking possibilities after graduation. Lastly, other factors beyond academic prestige are also important, such as your happiness and your success!

Both name and fit may be important to you. But, given the distinction between "name" and "fit" described here, where would you put yourself on the following continuum? Your position may change over the college planning process, but for now, rate yourself on this factor based on where you stand today.

The "name" or prestige of a college is most important in my college search.	1	2	3	4	5	The fit of the college (social and academic atmosphere, size) is most important in my college search.

Quality 12—Admission Difficulty

Consider what you learned about yourself in *Chapter 2*. Think about the level of difficulty of your courses and the extent of your curiosity, independence, and organization. Review the results of *Worksheet 4, Your Admission/Readiness Profile.*

When you compare yourself with others in your own high school graduating class, where do you think you stand? What level of admission difficulty do you feel you fit into? Being realistic is essential here.

The most selective colleges are appropriate for me.	1	2	3	4	5	Less selective colleges are appropriate for me.

Quality 13—Location

The first task here is to decide the relative weight of location in your college selection. Is location more important than other factors such as overall quality of the college and its academic offerings, size, or cost? Or is location a relatively low consideration on your college choice list? Do you want to attend school close to home? Will you want to come home often? (Even the least homesick student may want to come home occasionally.)

Location is the most important factor in choosing a college.	1	2	3	4	5	Other factors are more important than location in choosing a college.
I'd like a college that is close to home.	1	2	3	4	5	Closeness to home is not particularly important to me.

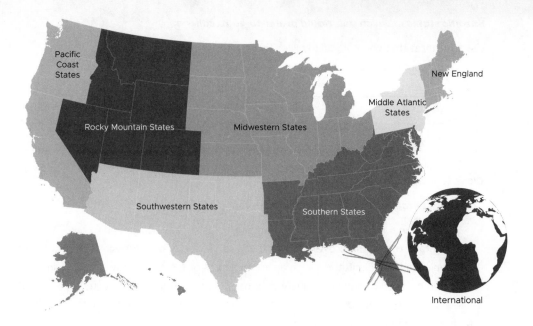

Think about the following in regard to the location of your college:

Regions of the country where you would prefer to go to college

Are some parts of the country or world more appealing than others? Do you prefer certain types of climates?

How concerned are you or your parents about the ease and expense of traveling to and from the college? Do you have relatives or close friends in particular states that you would like to be near? (A relative or friend can be a valuable support system when you're away from home for the first time.)

Keep in mind that you're choosing an academic environment where you will spend four years—you are not choosing a vacation site! Referring to the regional boundaries as defined on the map on the opposite page, ***circle those regions of the country you will consider in choosing a college:***

| Pacific Coast | Rocky Mountain | (Middle Atlantic) | Midwestern |
| Southwestern | (New England) | Southern | International |

—only coast near not Florida

Specific states in which you would prefer to go to college:

List any states that you particularly like. Try not to think of specific colleges within a given state, but rather think about states where you would enjoy going to college.

_____

_____

_____

Close to a city?

Consider the following three possibilities:

1. **A college in a major city.** Being in a medium or large city allows you to take advantage of a number of amenities. If you follow major or professional sports teams or enjoy cultural institutions such as art museums or the symphony, a college in a city or nearby suburb may best satisfy your needs. Will you go crazy if you don't have at least one large shopping mall and several movie theaters within 15 minutes of your dorm? Then this option will be best.

2. **A college near a large city, but not in it.** These colleges are located on the outskirts of the city or in the outer suburbs. With this option, students have access to a city but also enjoy a campus with a distinct "feel" that often includes large, grassy areas.

3. **A college in a small town or a rural location.** If you prefer a more serene or relaxed college atmosphere, a tranquil location such as a rural college in a small college town may suit you best. Such colleges may be one or two hours or more from a medium to large city. Typically, the towns in which these colleges are located show great support for college students and their activities. Store owners may call you by name and cash your check without identification. In small towns, many of the services (pizza places, dry cleaners, etc.) cater to students. Furthermore, colleges farther away from a city tend to go to great lengths to bring concerts, speakers, and other programs to the campus.

Which of these options sound appealing to you as you think about the kind of place in which you will be comfortable? Check any or all that apply:

_____✓_____ 1. In a major city *maybe* *maybe not*

_____✓_____ 2. Near a large city, but not in it

_____ 3. In a small town or a rural location
(or where the college is the focus of the town)

Are there any other location factors that are important to you? For example, do you want to be near a beach or close to outdoor/nature activities (hiking, streams, mountains, kayaking, etc.)? Are you a city person who thrives in the downtown of a big metropolis? *Use the space provided to note any other location characteristics that matter to you.*

TREES!!!!!! LOTS OF TREES!

Quality 14—Academic Success in College

Look carefully at all the factors you've identified as being important to your search for "best fit" colleges. Is there anything else a college could provide to help you accomplish your academic goals and do your best? For example, if you need quiet in order to study well, you may want to check whether a college's residential halls have spaces set aside for this purpose; after all, depending on time of day or weather conditions, you may not find it convenient or feasible to head to the library every time you want to study. It might be worth investigating the possibility of whether single occupant rooms are available to freshmen and at what additional cost, if any. If you prefer studying with others, many colleges offer guidelines and suggestions for forming a study group that is effective and productive for all members.

Would you be reluctant to go to the college's academic advising office with questions about courses, professors, or grading? Then look for schools that have a strong peer academic advisor program; these students, who have demonstrated their ability to handle the academic load at their school, can give you the inside scoop on the best courses and professors (as well as directions to the closest all-night coffee shop). Make a list of these and any other factors that you feel will affect your academic success in college.

Your academic success is also influenced by your desire to be in college. Are you not only prepared but eager to go to college immediately after high school? Or have you found yourself wondering about taking a gap year or working for a year before enrolling? A student who is self-motivated to attend college will be the most successful. And sometimes that self-motivation may lead a young person to postpone college to explore the working world or a particular interest before resuming academic endeavors. *On your list of items necessary for academic success, include whether you have made the decision to go to college by yourself and/or whether you'd like to consider taking a year off between high school and college.*

_____

_____

_____

_____

_____

_____

_____

Quality 15—Fitting In/Being Comfortable in College

Again, look carefully at the factors you have said are important in choosing your college. Are there other qualities a college could provide that would lead to your overall comfort with your college? If you were to visit a college tomorrow, is there anything else you would ask about or look for in addition to those factors you listed on this worksheet? **_List any additional factors below. Examples include a large number of days of sunshine (or snow), access to public transportation, a lively music scene, or space for a hobby in your dorm room._**

_____

_____

_____

_____

_____

_____

Worksheet 6—Characteristics of Your Ideal College

By completing **Worksheet 5**, you have considered fifteen qualities or characteristics important to you in selecting a college. In the spaces below, summarize what you have discovered about the qualities you seek and their importance. More specifically, review your responses to each of the fifteen qualities. Then select the eight most important features of a college and write statements summarizing what you are looking for in a college. The following examples may help you.

Examples:

1. It is very important for me to have a balance between academics and social life. I don't want a pressure-cooker college!
2. Cost is a significant factor for me and my family. I should pay particular attention to colleges that either cost less or where I might be eligible for some type of scholarship.
3. I'm looking for a small college because I seek contact with professors and opportunities to get involved in lots of athletic activities. Size of the college is very important to me.
4. All locations are okay with me, but my preference is for colleges on the west coast or in New England.
5. I'm looking for a liberal arts and sciences college because I'm still deciding on a career.
6. Words that describe ideal peers in college are artsy, creative, spontaneous, and liberal.
7. Although it's not imperative, I would prefer a college with many Catholic students.
8. I'd like a college whose students care about the environment.

Top 8 Characteristics of Your Ideal College

1. _____

_____

_____

_____

2. _____

_____

_____

_____

3. _____

_____

_____

_____

4. _____

_____

_____

_____

5. _____

_____

_____

_____

6. _____

_____

_____

_____

7. _____

_____

_____

_____

8. _____

_____

_____

_____

Chapter 4 focuses on learning about strategies that will help meet the cost of college. In **Chapter 5**, you will identify, then compare, the colleges that meet your now-established criteria.

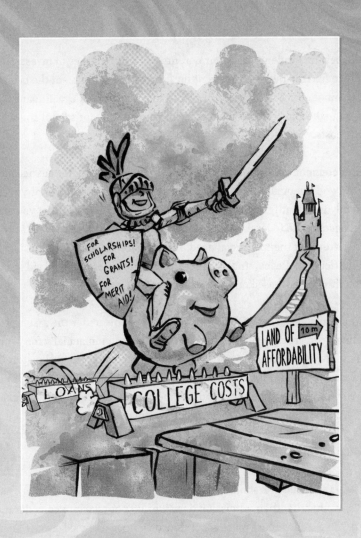

Chapter 4

Paying For College—Deal With It; Don't Run From It

Introduction

Choosing a college is a family endeavor. This chapter is geared toward parents because they are the ones who typically plan for and/or pay for their son or daughter's education. Thus, the "you" on these pages refers to parents. That said, however, it is essential that your student be engaged in cost discussions as well.

Students need to be "cost-conscious" as they consider their college options. And everyone should keep in mind that a more expensive college, or even one that is more selective, is not necessarily the best fit. Students and their parents working together to investigate colleges are more likely to find the best environment for growth and success—at the best price. Most families cannot afford to pay the full cost of four years of college. Financial aid is designed to bridge the gap between what you can afford to pay for school and what the school actually costs.

One of the most common college planning mistakes is not applying for aid because you assume that you will not qualify. However, there are several reasons to apply, even if you doubt your family will qualify. First, you may be surprised to discover that you are eligible for assistance. Second, the federal government sponsors some loans that are available to all students regardless of their financial need or their parents' finances. Third, in certain states and at particular colleges, students must have applied for financial aid in order to be considered for either need-based or non-need-based aid.

Another common mistake is to consider only in-state schools under the assumption that the cost of attending a private college or university is out of reach financially for your family. In fact, many of these colleges may provide significant aid. For example, Princeton University reports that the average grant for a student from a family earning $250,000 or above is almost $20,000. More generally, there is no income cut-off to qualify for federal student aid. Many factors are taken into consideration as colleges make these decisions. Parents are wise to contact several colleges, use web resources and net price calculators to determine their prospects for aid.

That said, parents and students should recognize that only a handful of colleges are totally "need-blind," meaning that their admission decisions do not take into consideration family financial need. Many colleges are more accurately described as "need-aware" in that financial need is a factor at some point—usually later—in the admission process. It may be true that on some level, parents who have the resources to pay for their student's education are more likely to see their son or daughter admitted; however, the relationship between college admission and ability to pay is limited at best. Many, many variables are taken into consideration as admission decisions are being made, and ability to pay is hardly a guarantee of acceptance. Yes, there is a risk that applying for aid may have an influence on one's admissibility, but the greater risk is that a student goes off to college without the necessary financial stability to be happy or successful. It makes little sense for a student to be admitted to a school but unable to attend due to finances. Even worse would be to attend and incur a financial cost that adversely affects the student's and the family's style of living for years to come. The bottom line is, if your family needs financial aid to cover college costs, apply for it. There are many quality colleges that are affordable and there is a lot of financial aid available. Your task is to help your student find these schools and try to secure financial aid to attend them. Pursuing financial aid opportunities as you and your student look for a good-choice college will be time-consuming but worth the effort. As important as financial aid is, you and your student should also be aware that financing college often means borrowing money and having a campus job.

Ultimately, when your student receives her or his admission decisions from each college, your family must weigh such variables as intellectual fit, social fit, and financial fit to arrive at your student's best educational option at the best price.

With regard to financial fit, make sure that you compare schools based on the net price. The net price will be the difference between the total cost of attendance—tuition and room and board, if applicable—and gift aid (grants and scholarships). This is the amount you will have to pay from savings, income, and loans to cover college costs.

As you and your child go about the process of investigating schools and assembling a college list, it may be difficult to make accurate cost comparisons without having your family's financial aid package and your student's scholarship offers in hand. This is why the wisest course for any household concerned about paying for college is to seek out colleges that are just as good as the "name" schools but cost less. It is worth mentioning here that applying via a binding early decision plan doesn't allow comparisons of financial aid packages.

Need-Based Aid

"Need-based aid" is the federal term for aid offered to a family because of family income/assets. Families who qualify for need-based aid are not necessarily "needy." Given the high cost of higher education today, most families qualify for some type of need-based aid even if they are living comfortably and enjoying a high quality of life.

Most colleges require you to complete the Free Application for Federal Student Aid (FAFSA) as the standardized need analysis form. Some colleges may require the College Scholarship Service (CSS) Financial Aid Profile. Several hundred colleges require that the CSS Profile be completed in addition to the FAFSA. Other colleges have their own financial aid applications. To make the matter even more cumbersome, some states have developed their own financial aid forms that are used in the awarding of state grants.

The FAFSA is the gateway to financial aid from the federal and state governments and most colleges and universities. You can file the FAFSA online at studentaid.gov/h/apply-for-aid/fafsa.

To help you determine your eligibility as determined by the FAFSA, calculators for your Expected Family Contribution (EFC) are available at
- https://www.savingforcollege.com/calculators/financial-aid-calculator
- https://finaid.org/calculators/
- https://vanguard.wealthmsi.com/csp.php (College savings planner)
- https://collegecost.ed.gov/net-price
  (US Department of Education Net Price Calculator Center)

The Net Price Calculator is designed to help you get a sense of whether your family will qualify for financial aid and what your student might pay at most colleges. Most every college provides a Net Price Calculator on their website. Some schools use the federal calculator, and some choose to use a calculator specific to that school. The U.S. Department of Education's College Affordability and Transparency Center (collegecost.ed.gov) has general information about the cost of college as well as a Net Price Calculator to estimate college costs.

The EFC has traditionally been based on family size, total income, assets, and number of children in college. The amount of your contribution is subtracted from the college costs to determine "need." For example, a family earning $150,000 with a child attending an in-state public university may not qualify for aid. A family earning $250,000 with two children attending private colleges probably will. While the cost of attendance varies from school to school, your federal EFC does not change on the basis of the school you attend. Information taken into consideration by federal, state, and individual college officials is often a work-in-progress. That is, guidelines change, and families need to contact colleges of interest directly to verify the factors considered. Finally, college financial aid is provided for one year only. So keeping up with financial aid matters is essential for parents throughout their student's college enrollment.

Be aware that different colleges may calculate your EFC very differently from the federal EFC, particularly if a college requires the CSS Profile. At certain colleges, the CSS Profile is used to determine the amount of nonfederal aid to be awarded to a student. College aid policies at each individual college can cause the calculated EFC to differ by thousands of dollars. The best estimate of possible financial aid might be obtained by using the Net Price Calculator on the website for a particular college, especially for those colleges requiring the CSS Profile.

Although getting financial aid is, in some ways, a mechanical process, it is also true that the financial aid officer at each college on your student's apply list plays a crucial role. Be sure to inform financial aid administrators about atypical expenses or unusual financial circumstances. Unusual financial circumstances may include anything that has changed from the tax year on which the FAFSA and CSS Profile are based or any circumstance that differentiates your family from the typical family. Examples include job loss, salary reductions, illness or death of a wage earner, substantial dependent care expenses for a special needs child or elderly parent, and high unreimbursed medical or dental expenses. When you are notified of how much financial aid your family will receive from a college, prepare for a "package"—and possibly a shortfall. If your student qualifies for aid from a college, don't expect all of it to be in the form of grants or gift aid. Gift aid refers to dollars given to a student without strings attached. Almost all need-based aid is given in a package consisting of some combination of these components: a grant (funds given to a student without a repayment obligation), a subsidized student loan (subsidized means interest does not have to be paid while the student attends college), and work-study (money earned through an on-campus job). Furthermore, because of tight financial aid budgets at most colleges, expect that the total amount of aid given will fall short of the amount for which you are eligible. This shortfall is called the "gap," meaning the amount you will have to provide in addition to your calculated EFC.

It is important to note that the financial aid process is not over once you have received a financial aid package. If the "gap" is too large to be affordable and unusual financial circumstances need to be further explained or new circumstances have arisen, you can, and should, appeal to a college's financial aid office. SwiftStudent, a resource listed at the end of this chapter, can aid in the process of requesting a change to your financial aid package. Also, be mindful that although your financial situation in any given year is consistent, colleges vary in the package they award your student. That is, College A might provide more grant money and fewer loans whereas College B offers fewer dollars in grants and more availability of loans.

Independent financial aid advisors not associated with an individual college are available, but few families really need to hire one. Basic questions can be answered by any number of financial aid books and websites (see "Useful Resources" at the end of this chapter) and/or by high school college counselors and financial aid officers at colleges. You might find the services of an advisor helpful if you need overall strategies to achieve your financial goals and objectives, including specific recommendations in areas such as cash management, debt liquidation, insurance coverage, and investment planning.

Changes to the FAFSA

The FAFSA Simplification Act of 2020 goes into effect in a few years. The Act streamlines the FAFSA by reducing the number of questions on the form and better aligns it to federal tax returns to decrease the amount of time it takes to fill out.

The Act will replace the Expected Family Contribution (EFC) with the Student Aid Index (SAI). Like the EFC, the SAI will be used to calculate need for most need-based aid programs. The major differences between the EFC and SAI will be the criteria used to calculate need and an expansion of the range of need values. While the EFC is determined on the basis of family size, total income, assets, and number of children in college, the SAI will be determined on the basis of family size, total income, and assets. In other words, having multiple children in college at the same time will no longer help families qualify for aid. Another difference between the EFC and the SAI is that the EFC cannot go below zero dollars; however, the SAI will allow negative numbers (down to -$1,500) in order to better represent students with the most financial need. A negative SAI will allow students with the greatest need to receive aid beyond the Cost of Attendance (COA) and will help states and institutions allocate need-based aid more effectively.

In addition, the Act will update the COA to be more inclusive of associated college costs. The updated COA will include tuition and fees, room and board, course materials, transportation, personal expenses, loan fees, and costs associated with obtaining professional licensure or certification. The Act will require that the itemized COA established by each institution be disclosed on the institution's website.

One notable need-based aid program that currently uses the EFC for award determination but will not use the SAI for award determination is Federal Pell Grants. Under the Act, there will be a separate process for Pell Grants based on household size and student adjusted gross income. Pell lookup tables will be made available for students to preview their eligibility for a Pell Grant.

Merit Aid, Scholarships, and Other Tuition Assistance

"Merit aid" refers to grants, scholarships, and discounts that a college awards to an admitted student not on the basis of demonstrated financial need. Merit awards are primarily granted by individual colleges and universities on the basis of a student's special accomplishments or skills (academic record, demonstrated leadership, musical or artistic ability, athletic prowess) or because the student represents a demographic (geographic region, alumni relative) that the college is eager to include in its enrollment. According to Lynn O'Shaughnessy, author of the blog The College Solution, 73% of college scholarships come from the colleges themselves.

In all but the wealthiest families where college costs are simply another household expense, students have an obligation to find colleges where they may be eligible for merit aid. To do this, students sometimes will have to broaden their college search and consider lesser-known schools, colleges in a location other than one they prefer, or small schools that are likely to have more merit aid available. Remember, the "perfect" college for your student could be the one that wants your daughter or son enough to help foot the bills there.

Students should contact the financial aid office of the schools that interest them and inquire whether the college offers merit scholarships, how and when to apply for that merit money, and whether a separate application is required. Many merit scholarships are awarded at the same time that the college reviews the student's admission papers and reflect the level of interest the college has in enrolling your son or daughter. Some merit scholarships within a college may be school-specific, i.e., available only to those intending to major in business, art or architecture, engineering, social work, or applied sciences. A careful search of the school's website should yield information on scholarships available as well as eligibility and requirements.

In addition to merit aid, many private scholarships are offered each year to prospective college students by a variety of corporate, professional, trade, government, civic, religious, social, and fraternal organizations. Any student whose PSAT score qualifies the student for a National Merit scholarship should devote the necessary effort to submit the required forms and essay (and, if a scholarship is awarded, the effort to renew the scholarship each year). For the student interested in a military career, the ROTC (Reserve Officer Training Corps) scholarship program represents another viable way of paying for college. Scholarships are also available for dependents of active duty or retired military personnel.

Private scholarships range in amount from small honorariums to thousands of dollars. The awards can be used at any college or university and may be sent to the student's college or be given directly to the student. There are scholarships for students who intend to enter specific fields or professions and for the offspring of parents in specific fields or professions. There are scholarships for students of certain ethnicities and for descendants of immigrants of various national heritages. And lastly, there are the "oddball" scholarships—the ones available only to left-handed students, golf caddies, or knitters.

Students are encouraged to apply for any scholarships for which they are both eligible and realistic candidates. At the same time, it is important to keep several factors front and center.

- First, the competition for scholarship money can be stiff, especially for larger awards. Even scholarships of $500 or less attract numerous applicants. Every dollar your student can secure will help defray costs, but consider how many awards of this amount (or less) will need to be cobbled together to cover just one semester of college expenses.
- Second, many scholarships are awarded for only a single year of college. The student may be limited to receiving only one scholarship or may need to reapply every year.
- Third, many scholarships come with stipulations such as maintaining a minimum GPA, serving in the military, or entering a specific field of study. In some cases, if the requirement is not met, the student may forfeit the scholarship or even be held liable for funds already spent.
- Fourth, unless your student already has the scholarship in hand, never count on scholarship awards to make up any shortfall in school fees.
- Lastly, check with the financial aid offices at the colleges on your student's list. Outside scholarships may reduce the amount of grant aid offered by a college.

You may come across companies that offer to search for aid or scholarships for your student. However, paying for such a service is seldom money well spent when you can easily sign up for any number of free search services. On a related note, beware of scholarship cons such as those that charge a fee to apply for the scholarship. More often than not, if you have to pay money to get money, it is probably a scam. Legitimate scholarship programs are open to everyone and seldom, if ever, charge a fee to apply.

In addition, beware of the "unclaimed aid" myth. It is not true that millions of dollars in scholarship money lie waiting for applicants. The money that goes unclaimed is most commonly money that is earmarked for ultra-specific student categories and thus not available to 90% of those planning for college attendance.

And lastly, an often-overlooked source of help with college costs is an employer tuition assistance program. Some corporations and businesses provide tuition assistance for not only their employees but also their employees' dependents and sometimes even grandchildren. Contact your company's Human Resources department about the availability of such benefits.

Tips on Timing

Start now. If you are reading this, you are engaged in college planning. That means you should be engaged in financial aid planning as well.

You may file the FAFSA and the CSS Profile as early as October 1 of your student's senior year in high school. After you file the FAFSA, you will receive a student aid report, which will contain your federal Expected Family Contribution. You should register for the CSS Profile (if required) at least two weeks before the earliest college or scholarship priority application date your student needs to meet. Experts suggest that families file at least by late October or early November because doing so will give them an early idea of their anticipated financial aid and college costs. If students apply for aid earlier in their senior year of high school, colleges can provide financial aid notifications to students earlier. Furthermore, some aid is awarded on a first-come, first-served basis for the following school year. The best advice on timing? Meet or beat the deadlines. Most colleges have limited aid budgets. When there is no money left, they stop giving aid.

The filing process calls for figures from the prior year's completed tax return (due the previous April) for both the FAFSA and the CSS Profile. The base year, i.e., the year on which college aid decisions for the first year of college are based, relies on information from January of the student's sophomore year of high school to December of the student's junior year.

It would be wise to acquire information about any necessary financial planning well before the base year. Families can submit a FAFSA using the IRS Data Retrieval Tool (DRT), allowing automatic population of a student's FAFSA with tax return data.

In the interim between the filing date of a family's base-year taxes and the time the student applies to colleges, a family's financial circumstances may worsen substantially. In this case, after filing the FAFSA using the base year required, you should contact the financial aid office at the schools on your student's apply list and provide the details of your current situation. This information is vital to helping financial aid officers assess your individual finances at the time of application and make any necessary adjustments to your EFC.

Keep in mind that need-based financial aid is typically for only one year. Students who are high school seniors apply for aid for their freshman year only. During their first year in college, these students reapply for aid to cover costs during their sophomore year and then continue to reapply each subsequent year. While some types of aid and grants continue beyond the first year, many do not.

The need analysis formulas are complicated enough that it is difficult to predict whether you will qualify unless you actually apply and reapply every year. Changes in income and amount of assets can have a big impact on aid eligibility. The amount of aid awarded to your family can also be affected by the number of children enrolled in college at same time. Be aware, however, that when the FAFSA Simplification Act takes effect on July 1, 2023, having multiple children in college at the same time will no longer help families in qualifying for aid. This should be a consideration if you expect to have more than one student in college at the same time.

Tips on Loans

Education debt is usually considered "good" debt because it is an investment in your student's future. However, each family must determine for itself how much education debt is acceptable.

Do your research before applying for a loan. Should you borrow from yourself and apply for a second mortgage or home equity loan? Life insurance policies may allow you to borrow against their cash value. Some 401(k) plans have a provision to allow account holders to withdraw money, but the money must be repaid within a relatively short timeframe. Is it possible to borrow money from extended family at a lower interest rate?

Federal student loans are cheaper, are more available, and have better repayment terms than private student loans. In addition, federal student loans are eligible for income-based repayment and public service loan forgiveness, whereas private student loans are not. While private student loans offer the advantage — or is it a disadvantage? — of unlimited loan amounts, they also come with higher interest rates and more restrictive repayment terms than other options. Some experts suggest turning to private lenders only as a last resort.

It may be common sense, but it is important enough to emphasize here: only borrow as much as your student needs. Higher education is best viewed as an investment much like a house, a car, or a share of stock. Its worth depends on the skills and motivation of the primary user: your son or daughter. Good advice is to finance one's education, not one's lifestyle. In other words, borrow for tuition and modest living, not for a private residence hall room or an unneeded computer. Don't overlook the possibility that your student may need additional loans to complete his or her degree or to attend graduate school.

Another smart piece of advice is to try to keep student loan debt in sync with the student's earning potential after graduation. Some young professionals in lower-paying fields find themselves having to postpone buying homes or starting families because they are still paying off their student loans. The Bureau of Labor Statistics offers a helpful salary estimator at https://www.bls.gov/bls/blswage.htm.

You also should recognize that both you and your child might have loans to repay. Your ability to repay and your child's ability to repay are likely to differ significantly. While the student's ability to repay a loan may be affected by the profession he or she chooses, age may be a factor in the parent's ability to repay. Parents who sacrifice a retirement nest egg to finance education costs run the risk of becoming a burden to their child.

Do not treat loan limits as targets. You can and should borrow less than the amount allowed under the annual and aggregate loan limits. Many financial aid experts believe that the student's total loan debt at graduation should be less than the student's projected annual starting salary in his or her field.

Find out what the expected monthly payments will be once the loan is in repayment. Typically, the loan payment schedule will be calculated automatically and attached to the loan when it is granted.

Before you and your student spend student loan money on anything, ask yourselves whether you'd still buy it at twice the price, because realistically, that's what it will cost you. Every dollar you spend in student loan money may cost your family about two dollars when you repay the debt.

Cost-Saving Strategies to Consider in Compiling a College List

Financial aid decisions and scholarship awards are out of your control. However, there are approaches that families can utilize to reduce college fees.

One of the most effective ways for a young person to reduce college costs is to enroll at an in-state public college. If your student chooses this option, be sure that she or he is mindful of the necessity of graduating in four years. Studies have found that because of limited enrollment in some required classes, some students at very large universities are unable to take the courses they need to graduate on time and may require an extra year to graduate, thus reducing the cost advantage of attending a public university. When visiting a college, ask what percentage of students graduate in four years, particularly in your student's study areas of interest.

Living at home during college, especially if the student attends an in-state public college, can save thousands of dollars. Every college website breaks down the cost of tuition and the cost of room and board, which makes it easy to calculate the potential cost savings over four years.

Families can save thousands of dollars if a student starts at a community college and then transfers to a four-year school. Many states have strong articulation agreements under which students who graduate from a state's community college with an associate's degree are guaranteed admission to one of the state's four-year public colleges.

Groups of states work together to make costs lower for students. For example, students in western states may enroll in many two-year and four-year college programs at a reduced tuition level through the Western Undergraduate Exchange (wiche.edu/wue). Many (but typically not all) undergraduate majors are available to students at participating colleges and universities; however, students may need to meet certain grade average requirements to qualify for the tuition discount. Similar programs are available in other parts of the U.S., such as the Midwest Student Exchange Program (msep.mhec.org) and the Academic Common Market (sreb.org/academic-common-market) for students from many southern states. High school college counselors can be a good source of information about these programs.

Another way to cut college costs is to reduce the amount of time needed to complete a degree. High school students can earn college credit through participation in programs such as International Baccalaureate (IB), Advanced Placement (AP), College-Level Examination Program (CLEP), and Proficiency Examination Program (PEP) tests. Students may have the opportunity to take dual enrollment classes, where high school students take college classes, either at their own high school or on a college campus. Students who enter college with sufficient college credits may be able to graduate in three years. This option may work well for the young person who is highly motivated and eager to begin a career or pursue an advanced degree. Some colleges offer programs that streamline requirements, which may allow a student to save a year's tuition. Examples include programs that combine a bachelor's degree with a master's degree in business or those that accelerate preparation for medical school by cutting one year from undergraduate studies.

Since the majority of scholarships and grants come from the colleges themselves, many families would be wise to investigate colleges where the student is likely to receive the most aid. In very general terms and depending on the cost of a college, families with a low EFC should look at colleges that provide generous need-based aid. If cost is a consideration for families with a high EFC, they should look at colleges that are generous with merit aid. Websites that are particularly helpful in this area include: collegedata.com, bigfuture.collegeboard.org/pay-for-college/paying-your-share, thecollegesolution.com, diycollegerankings.com, road2college.com, and collegeresults.org.

College savings plans, such as 529 plans, are worth investigating as well. Earnings in a 529 plan grow federal tax-free and will not be taxed when the money is taken out to pay for college. Depending on the state, there may be state tax benefits available as well. As these are investments that can grow over time, families want to start contributing as early as possible.

Be aware that the FAFSA taxes parent assets at up to 5.6% per year, and the CSS Profile taxes parent assets at 5%. However, student assets are taxed at the maximum rate by the FAFSA at 20% per year and the CSS Profile at 25% per year. So it may be beneficial to move money from a student account to a parent account before filing the FAFSA or CSS Profile. The amount in bank accounts that will be considered is the amount in the account on the date that the FAFSA or CSS Profile is filed.

Keep in mind that whether or not these strategies will be useful to your family will depend on your student's choice of colleges. Some schools may require students to live on campus their first year. Not all colleges accept AP and IB credit in the same way. Some colleges place limits on the number of outside college credits they will accept. Others require you to take a certain number of courses at their institution to graduate. For regional consortiums of states offering discounted tuition, the key word is "participating"; not all colleges within these regions are members of their respective programs. If one or more of these strategies looks promising, your student's prospective list of colleges will need to include schools where these options are available.

Cost-Saving Strategies to Consider While Enrolled in College

The goal of this book is to help high school students find a college that's a great match, intellectually, socially, and financially. However, ensuring that the great matchup between student and school continues throughout the student's college career is equally important.

College costs are not stagnant and likely will increase during the years your son or daughter is enrolled. Furthermore, family finances can change unexpectedly, and money once available to pay school fees may have to be directed toward other expenses. Students need to be mindful of their financial responsibility while in college, and parents need to take time to talk frankly with their student about college expenses. Both students and their parents should look at ways the student can save money while attending college.

The most obvious way for students to significantly lower their college costs is to be good managers of their money and their time. Keeping track of how money is spent can help a student plug the holes in the budget where cash is going to frivolous or unnecessary expenses. Tracking how time is spent is just as important. Hours spent texting, surfing the Internet, or playing video games mean less time for studies and could eliminate the possibility of part-time work.

Your son or daughter can earn money for college by working part-time during the school year and/or full-time during the summer. Even if a student doesn't qualify for the Federal Work-Study aid program, part-time jobs are usually plentiful on or near college campuses. Studies have shown that rather than taking away from the student's scholastic work, working ten to twelve hours a week during the semester can help improve student grades, because the student must be more organized and focused.

Some colleges provide free or greatly reduced room and board to students who work as Head Residents or Resident Assistants in campus residence halls. Some schools pay students who hold leadership positions in student activities, such as president of the student body or editor of the student newspaper.

Students who have demonstrated the ability to handle their course load and budget their time effectively should consider taking an extra class each semester and classes during the summer semester in order to graduate more quickly. Some colleges do not charge extra tuition for taking a heavier academic load and/or charge lower tuition during the summer semester. Another strategy for saving on tuition would be to take classes during the summer at a local community college, where costs are less. However, the student should be sure to verify ahead of time that his or her school will give full credit for the course.

It is important to note that changing academic majors or transferring from one college to another can increase the time, and therefore cost, to complete a bachelor's degree. Though credits can be transferred, basic requirements are not always the same from school to school. For this reason, if cost is a big concern, students should be certain of their choices before changing majors and transferring to another school.

Once enrolled in college, students need not give up on their search for scholarship money. An online search for scholarships yields numerous awards available to currently enrolled students. Students should not overlook scholarship opportunities that may be on their own campus. In addition to its four-year scholarship program for high school students, ROTC offers three-year and two-year scholarships for those already attending college. Some colleges and universities award scholarships within specific majors as the student advances. Students should check with their individual colleges and departments for details.

While your daughter or son explores options to lower college costs, you can do your part as well. One approach is to take advantage of tuition prepayment discounts if available. Colleges may offer up to a 10% discount for early payment. If prepayment is not an option, be sure and pay college fees on time because late payments may incur substantial penalties.
Another option is to consider tuition installment plans as a less expensive alternative to student loans. Tuition installment plans allow you to pay the college bills in monthly or semiannual installments over the academic year. Tuition installment plans do not charge interest but may charge a modest sign-up fee.

Getting Started: Useful Resources

Helpful books include:

- *How to Appeal for More College Financial Aid* by Mark Kantrowitz
- *How to Control Your College Costs: The Path to College Affordability* by C. Claire Law
- *Paying for College: Everything You Need to Maximize Financial Aid and Afford College* by Kalman Chany and Princeton Review
- *The College Solution* by Lynn O'Shaughnessy
- *The Other College Guide: A Roadmap to the Right School for You* by Jane Sweetland, Paul Glastris, and staff of Washington Monthly
- *The Price You Pay for College* by Ron Lieber
- *The Truth about College Admission: A Family Guide to Getting In and Staying Together* by Brennan Barnard and Rick Clark
- *The Ultimate College Financial Aid Guide* by Diana Barbu
- *Twisdoms About Paying for College* by Mark Kantrowitz

Here are a few useful websites:

- bigfuture.collegeboard.org (click on "Pay for College" for information on financial aid and college costs; provides tips and advice on financial aid and includes the CSS Profile online, the application used by many colleges in calculating need)
- collegecostnavigator.com (College Cost Navigator)
- collegedata.com (use the "College Match Search" with the Financials, Debt & Aid filters or the "College Match Search" to go a particular college's profile and look for factors need met, gift aid, debt, awards, time to graduate, and data for freshman vs. data for all undergraduates)
- collegefinanciallady.com (website with resources on the financial aid process)
- collegeresults.org (compares financial data across colleges)
- diycollegerankings.com (Do It Yourself College Rankings, emphasis on data)
- ed.gov (a government site with information on federal loans and grants)
- studentaid.gov/h/apply-for-aid/fafsa (Free Application for Federal Student Aid [FAFSA]) website)
- fafsa.ed.gov/spa/fafsa4c (FAFASA4caster estimates eligibility for federal student aid)
- finaid.org (provides a calculator to estimate the amount of aid you may receive, as well as assistance on navigating through the financial aid process)
- Google net price calculator (search name of college, net price calculator)
- nces.ed.gov/collegenavigator (National Center for Educational Statistics tool)
- road2college.com (advice on college admissions and financing)
- salliemae.com (student loan information and how to finance college education)
- studentaid.ed.gov (government site with lists of useful links)
- thecollegesolution.com (how to make college more affordable)
- formswift.com/swift-student (forms to use in appealing a financial aid award)

The following sites provide a free scholarship search service:

- bigfuture.collegeboard.org/scholarship-search
- cappex.com/scholarships
- edvisors.com
- fastaid.com
- fastweb.com
- finaid.org/scholarships/
- scholarships.com
- unigo.com/scholarships
- bold.org
- myscolly.com
- scholarshipowl.com
- chegg.com/scholarships
- niche.com/colleges/scholarships

There are also apps available via Apple Apps or Google Play that might be useful. Examples include myStudentAid (US Department of Education), ScholarshipOwl, RaiseMe, Scholarships.com, Going Merry, and Scholly.

Once the student has identified colleges to explore, be sure to check out the college's own website to find information on specific financial aid requirements, forms, and procedures.

Cost is an essential consideration for most college shoppers, and in this chapter, we considered ways of understanding and managing the financial side of college attendance. In the next chapter, we'll look at cost among other variables in building a college list that fits a student financially, socially, and educationally.

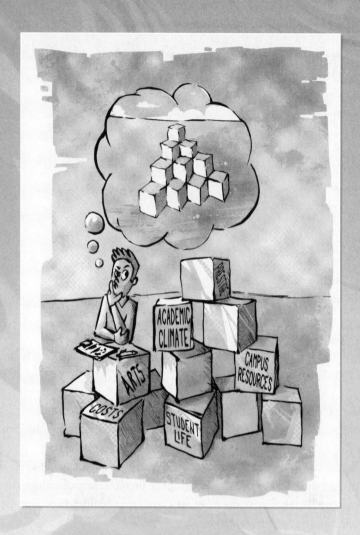

Chapter 5
Building Your College List

Now that you've learned more about yourself (*Chapter 2*) and identified the qualities that will make a college the right match for you (*Chapter 3*), and learned strategies to help deal with the cost of college (*Chapter 4*), your next step is to figure out which specific colleges best meet your background and talents, as well as those that come closest to matching the combination of factors you identified as important to your academic and social success. College planning involves three key decision points:

- determining which colleges to consider,
- choosing which colleges to apply to, and
- selecting the college to attend.

This chapter is intended to help you with the first two decision points.

Finding your college match might sound a bit overwhelming, given that you have more than 4,000 colleges to choose from. But this chapter guides you through a systematic analysis and review that should make the process quite doable. Remember that for every student, there are likely dozens of "good match" colleges. You're not hunting for the rare pearl in the oyster. In college planning, "pearls" are everywhere; they're just waiting for you to find them.

Arriving at Your Initial List of Colleges

Without knowing you or your goals, background, and interests, no one can draw up a list of specific colleges to which you should apply. What this chapter offers you is a plan for finding those colleges. Two items should be noted before you begin, however.

First, although your personal visits to colleges are a terrific source of information at various stages of your list-building process, campus visits are not discussed in this section because **Chapter 6** is devoted to this topic. Second, keep in mind that books go out of print and links to materials on the Internet change. Many books and websites are cited in this chapter in the hope that if one source of material is not available, another may be.

Top 12 Strategies for List-Building

Deciding on colleges to apply to takes time, patience, research skill, and determination. At the end of this section, you will list twenty colleges that seem right for you. How you arrive at this list depends on a number of factors, but the following eleven strategies should get you started. Not all of these strategies will be applicable to your individual search, and you may decide to do them in a different order.

1. *Use your high school counseling/career resources.* High school counseling offices are a key school resource in providing information about colleges. You should meet with your counselor as often as your school and your needs dictate. Talk with your counselor about your interests, providing as much information about yourself as is necessary for him or her to put together a list of recommended colleges that are right for you. Show your counselor the worksheets you completed in this book. Remember, however, that counselors are busy people, often with many different responsibilities. So be organized when you visit with your counselor, and come prepared with questions and issues for discussion. Your high school counseling/career office may also have materials such as guides, online resources, or college viewbooks. Also, be sure to check out college planning materials that may be available via your high school website.

2. *Go to admissions presentations when college representatives visit your high school.* Health permitting, admissions representatives from many colleges visit high schools for short, usually under-an-hour presentations about admissions and the college itself.

Check with your high school counseling office to see which representatives are visiting and how often. These representatives can give a face to a college you are interested in and help communicate the overall culture of the school as well other "intangibles" that cannot be found online or in a guidebook. These representatives are the most informed resources for your specific questions about issues such as majors and merit-based financial aid. Don't hesitate to ask questions and learn more.

3. *Go online and complete one or more of the college searches available.* Major college planning websites (collegedata.com, collegeresults.org, collegescorecard.ed.gov/, cappex. com, collegeboard.org, princetonreview.com, collegefactual.com and usnews.com) as well as others (unigo.com, petersons.com, colleges.niche.com, collegesimply.com, collegevine.com, and nces.ed.gov/collegenavigator) provide the means to input what you want in a college and then retrieve a list of potential schools. To search for colleges, you enter the basic facts that are relevant to you in selecting a college (such as major, location, or size), and the search returns a list of colleges that meet the criteria you have set. This can be a good first step, but keep in mind that such approaches are limited. No college search program can take into account all the factors that matter to you or weight them in order of importance. Only you can choose the exact college environment that is appropriate for you.

4. *Search general or specialized books focusing on colleges.* Check online booksellers, physical bookstores, and your local library for books focusing on the college planning areas that are most significant to you. You'll find books highlighting the most competitive colleges, "good value" colleges (see suggestions in **Chapter 4**), and colleges that are right for a B student (see *America's Best Colleges for B Students. Colleges That Change Lives* is a classic that gives descriptions of fine liberal arts and sciences colleges. Keep in mind that the 40 or so schools highlighted, while each is outstanding, are reflective of many other schools in the "small, liberal arts and sciences" category. If you are interested in particular states, go to one of the review guidebooks (for example, *Fiske Guide to Colleges or The Princeton Review: The Best Colleges*), and read the descriptions for colleges within those states. Even though these guides describe only a fraction of the colleges in each state, they are a good place to start. If you already have a few colleges in mind—maybe one a sibling or a friend attends—read about each college in one of the subjective guides. In the *Fiske Guide*, look at schools you are interested in and then check out "Overlap Schools." You can also use collegeresults.org by typing in the name of a college in the search bar. Once the page for the selected school has loaded, click on "Similar Colleges" to see other possibilities you may want to consider. This kind of information can help expand your initial list beyond schools that are familiar to you.

5. *Do a thorough web search.* For example, if you want to find colleges entrance test policies at fairtest.org. For descriptions of collections of colleges, explore Colleges of Distinction (collegesofdistinction.com) or Council on Public Liberal Arts Colleges

(coplac.org). If you are seeking a college with a religious affiliation, *there are books and websites for many religious groups (for example, Christian, Catholic, and Jewish*. Many websites—such as ldaamerica.org, wrightslaw.com, and ldonline.org—provide useful information for students with learning disabilities. You can even locate a college geographically by purchasing *U.S. College and University Reference Map* (hedberggroup.com). Use collegedata.com or College Navigator (nces.ed.gov/collegenavigator/) to get basic facts such as enrollment, over-all cost, percent of student's receiving merit based financial aid, average financial aid award, most popular majors, club sports offered, retention and graduation rates, etc.

6. ***Use social media platforms.*** Social media focusing on colleges and universities offers prospective students a wealth of information. Almost all colleges have social media managers, some of whom may coordinate several thousand social media sites. Social media managers are usually very responsive to questions and comments from followers, so this can be a great way to engage in a conversation about aspects of the college that interest you. Social media sites are proliferating. These platforms fall into five main categories: 1) social networking sites such as Facebook, Twitter, Google+, Clubhouse, Amino, etc.; 2) blogs such as Reddit, Tumblr, Quora, etc.; 3) image-sharing sites such as Instagram, Snapchat, Pinterest, Whisper, etc.; 4) video-sharing sites such as YouTube, Facebook Live, TikTok, Vimeo, Houseparty, Live.me, etc.; and 5) texting apps such as GroupMe, Kik Messenger, WhatsApp, Discord, Telegram, etc.

    For any admission-related information—admission process, guidelines, and deadlines—you'll want to rely on information that comes directly from the school's main site and the admission office. But you can explore a college's other social media accounts to find insights into individual academic departments, campus life, faculty, events and activities, athletics, music groups, dining halls, the fraternity/sorority scene, scholarships, research, and more. Keep in mind that any sites directly associated with the college will likely offer a somewhat curated view of the college. For less-filtered and potentially more-useful information, look for sites managed by students (campus newspaper), search for individual professors by name, or check out alumni groups in your hometown.

    Here are a few suggestions for effectively using social media to build your college list.
    *   A simple search on, for example, Pomona College, brings up a range of information—everything from the four-year graduation rate to notable alumni. This is a great place to start, but the more focused your search, the more you'll be able to find the info you're looking for.
    *   You can be fairly specific in your search terms, using such phrases as "Texas Christian University admissions," "University of Montana financial aid," "Physics at Carleton College," or "MIT Class of [insert recent year]."
    *   Remember that in addition to searching by words, you can use tags and hashtags to zero in on a topic.

- Different platforms allow you to use different search functions. On Twitter, a search on a college by name brings up tweets from any account mentioning that school.

- If you're interested in what's going on off campus or nearby, check out social media for the city or town where the college is located. You'll not only discover what kind of social, dining, or work opportunities exist off campus, you'll gain insight into town–gown relationships, i.e., how well students and locals interact and get along.

- Student blogs can provide an insider's look at a college as well as a means of connecting with current students. Search "[name of college] student blogs" and see what comes up. As with any individual social media accounts, you'll find those who are enthusiastic supporters of their school and others who have an axe to grind. When reading blog entries and comments, remember that these are individual perspectives.

- Much of social media—whether it's the university's official Facebook account or the glee club president's Twitter feed—focuses on the good, the successes, the wins. The reality is the campus is not always bathed in that autumn glow and the football team sometimes gets skunked.

- Social media can be a terrific tool for researching colleges, but it can also be a huge time sink. Start with a clear idea of what you want to know, and if you can't find a lead to that information within a reasonable amount of time, move on.

7. ***Check out the college planning apps available for your smartphone.*** A number of apps available in the App Store, Google Play, and elsewhere are designed to aid students in college planning. Try searching app stores or conduct a web search using the terms "college planning" or "college admission apps."

8. ***Talk with your parents.*** Your parents may have perspectives about schools they attended or know about through friends or relatives. This kind of input, when combined with other sources of information, can be helpful in choosing your college. Of course, you'll have to be on the lookout for comments that stereotype a college as "a party school," "a school for nerds," "not a 'good' school," etc. Listen to your parents' perceptions, but do your own research as well.

9. ***Talk with your friends.*** Ask friends who have just been through the college admission process for their impressions of colleges they are considering or attending. They may have researched schools similar to those you have in mind, or they may have recently visited a number of colleges and can share their impressions. Also, stay tuned to the "college grapevine" at your school or among your friends. Remember, however, that nobody knows your background and your feelings as well as you do. So listen attentively

but reserve final judgment until you investigate for yourself. One person's ideal college could be another person's collegiate disaster.

10. **Consider contacting a professional trained in the area of college admission planning.** Independent educational consultants are professionals who assist students in choosing a college. They offer knowledge about colleges (gained, in part, by traveling to dozens of colleges annually) as well as the time necessary to explore your situation in depth. You may want to ask about a consultant's membership in professional organizations and professional credentials. For a listing of educational consultants, contact the Independent Educational Consultants Association (IECA) at IECAonline.com or the Higher Education Consultants Association (HECA) at hecaonline.org. You may also want to ask if the consultant is a Certified Educational Planner (CEP). A directory of CEPs and other information about this credential (which requires a board-certified examination) are available at aicep.org.

11. **Read broadly and become acquainted with the current climate in colleges, college selection, and college admission.** For example, look at some of the general college planning books such as *The Truth about College Admission: A Family Guide to Getting In and Staying Together* by Barnard and Clark and *Admission Matters* by Springer, Reider, and Morgan. The website HowStuffWorks has webpages on How College Admissions Works (howstuffworks.com/college-admission) and How College Financial Aid Works (howstuffworks.com/college-financial-aid). Several highly respected authors offer invaluable insights into specific aspects of the college search and college admission process. Among them are two books by Loren Pope. One is *Colleges That Change Lives* and the other is *Looking Beyond The Ivy League*. Good sources of information about selective college admission is found in *Who Gets In and Why* by Jeffrey Selingo and *The Gatekeepers* by Jacques Steinberg. Frank Bruni provides valuable insights in *Where You Go Is Not Who You'll Be: An Antidote to the College Admissions Mania*. *The College Finder* (by this author) is a collection of lists of colleges in categories such as "Colleges With Excellent Programs in Biology," "Colleges With Great Study Abroad Programs," and "Colleges Where Students With Learning Disabilities Succeed."

12. **Start thinking about possible majors and careers.** As stated elsewhere in this book, to find a "good match" college, you do not need to know exactly what you will be when you grow up. Indeed, the process of career formulation takes time and experience and often develops as one moves through the college years. On the other hand, exploring interests and potential careers is a wise step for most students. The more options you consider, the more likely you will make the best ultimate career choice. High school students can benefit from taking a career inventory or gathering vocational information through research. Ask your high school counselor or independent educational consultant for resources in this area. Numerous books are available for those seeking information on a variety of academic and career fields such as visual and performing arts, journalism,

and creative writing. ***Appendix J, References for College Planning***, lists several career-oriented books.

You can complete the worksheets found in *What Color Is Your Parachute for Teens* by Christen and Bolles), or purchase and use *StrengthsFinders*, a comprehensive yet accessible source of career advice. Or try googling the name of your proposed major. O*NET (onetonline.org) is a comprehensive career resource. Other websites worth checking are California Career Zone assessments (cacareerzone.org/assessments), Career Cluster Interest Survey (iseek.org/careers/clusterSurvey), Focus 2 Assessment (focus2career.com), MyMajors (mymajors.com), My Next Move (mynextmove.org), Strengths Mining (strengthsmining.com), Bureau of Labor Statistics (stats.bls.gov). Finally, Carleton College has a useful visualization tool (apps.carleton.edu/career/visualize/). It lets you see the final career destination for those who majored in each specific major.

Incorporating Your Personal Criteria into the Search

Having gone through the work of identifying what you want in a college, now you need to make sure that you incorporate your personal search criteria into your search for "good match" colleges. On **Worksheet 5** you identified the qualities that you considered important and unimportant in a college. On **Worksheet 6**, you listed the eight characteristics of your ideal college. Each of these characteristics represents one dimension of your search. One might have to do with size or location. One might relate to religious preference, academic interest, or some other factor. These are the building blocks you use to construct your list of colleges. Now use some of the ten strategies described previously to find colleges that meet your personal criteria.

Here are some examples:
- If you are looking mainly at in-state colleges, your high school counseling office is often the best place to go for the most up to date information on application procedures and programs.
- If you are seeking a Catholic college and would like to be on the West coast, use any of the guidebooks mentioned in this chapter (or do an online search for Catholic colleges) to identify Catholic schools in California, Oregon, Washington, and other states you are considering.
- If you are an African-American student, check out Black Excel: The College Help Network (blackexcel.org) or United Negro College Fund (uncf.org). If you are Hispanic/Latino, visit the website of The Hispanic Association of Colleges and Universities (hacu.net).
- If you want a Division III women's lacrosse program, go to a site such as ncaa.com and look at colleges sorted by conference.

- While campus safety is important, data on campus safety and security are often inaccurate due to underreporting or other factors. Studies show that the safest colleges are those with 10,000 to 20,000 students in a city with a population under 100,000. The colleges most prone to violent crime are those with fewer than 10,000 students in a city with populations of more than 500,000. The size of the town or city is often the best predictor of violent crime on campus.
- Did your worksheet indicate that cost is a key consideration in your college search? If so, check out the resources listed at the end of **Chapter 4**.
- There's a wealth of information through the University and College Accountability Network (ucan-network.org) developed by the National Association of Independent Colleges and Universities. Here you can find information and profiles of some 900 private, nonprofit colleges and universities participating in the network. Another resource is the Council of Independent Colleges (cic.edu), with over 700 college members.

Final Advice

By now you should have a fairly good idea of what you want in a college. You have talked to your advisor about college possibilities, you have received input from your parents and solicited suggestions from other people who know you. You may have e-mailed or written for information from the colleges that interest you.

On **Worksheet 7**, you will create your list of colleges that you are considering. These are schools that you will investigate in depth in order to determine where you will submit an application. The worksheet provides 20 spaces; your list may have 5 colleges or 40 colleges. Whatever the size of the list, this is where your comparisons of colleges begins.

As you decide on which schools to include, think about two components that are essential to finding your match colleges:

- **Academic Factors:** Where will I be challenged but not overwhelmed? Where am I going to be able to get the best grades? Where will I learn the most? Where is the learning environment that best fits my own learning style?
- **Social Factors:** Where am I going to be comfortable? Where will I fit in? Where am I likely to make lots of friends?

At this point in the process. . .
- Do not focus too much on major.
- Do not focus too much on cost.
- Do not focus too much on location.
- Do not focus too much on prestige.

Because this is a preliminary list, you don't want to rule out any college too soon. At the same time, you do need to take into account your personal situation. For example, cost may be a primary concern for your family. Look for colleges that meet the financial needs of their students. Search for colleges that offer lots of merit scholarships (most of that information is available on the web). Seek out schools that are just as good but cost less. As you arrive at a list of colleges to consider, the idea is to not let one factor, such as finances, overshadow other characteristics, such as location, size, or type of student.

Worksheet 7—Colleges You Are Considering

Name of College	Name of College
1.	11.
2.	12.
3.	13.
4.	14.
5.	15.
6.	16.
7.	17.
8.	18.
9.	19.
10.	20.

Comparing Your College Choices

Worksheet 7 lists colleges that have made your "first cut." The next step involves researching these schools with the goal of arriving at the final list of colleges to which you will apply. **Worksheet 8, College Fact Finder**, asks you for answers to specific aspects of the colleges on your list and provides spaces for you to fill in the results of your research. The four forms provided can accommodate your comments on a dozen schools. If you are researching more than twelve colleges, make copies of this worksheet.

Below is a brief look at the components of **Worksheet 8**; specific steps guiding you though completion of the form can be found later in this chapter:

— You are asked to indicate where the college is located and how you will get there. For example, is it within driving distance? Will you be able to take a nonstop flight?

— In the next space, you will write down the number of students enrolled.

— Note whether the college offers the academic programs you seek. Remember, however, that you don't need to know exactly what your career will be; what you are looking for is an academic environment where you can grow and learn about your career options. If you don't have a specific career in mind, comment on whether the college seems like a good place to explore. For example, does it seem easy to change majors? To find out, see what the college website says (if anything) about being undecided or ask the college representative what resources are available to students who are still deciding on a major. Are graduates being hired in a wide variety of fields?

— Your perceptions of "life outside of class" are essential to finding a good college match; after all, you'll be spending the next years of your life in this environment. Look at the "student life" section of the college's website to see the clubs offered, the status of fraternities and sororities, intramural sports opportunities, and so on. You'll find more suggestions for researching student life later in this chapter.

— You are asked to list one positive and one negative feature about the college. All colleges have both!

— You are also asked whether the college is a high-, medium-, or low- chance-of-admission school for you. The discussion that begins on page 96 provides guidelines to use for determining your likelihood of admission.

— The cost of attending a college is found in most guidebooks and on the college website. Be sure you obtain comparable data (including room and board, fees, etc.) for each school. In addition, each college posts a net price calculator on its website to provide estimated net price information to current and prospective students and their families.

— Use the last space to describe something else that struck you about the college. This "something else" might be sports available, religious or ethnic considerations, merit scholarship opportunities, or any other factor you feel is important to remember about the college. Is there any additional information you'd like to know about the college?

— At the end of your review, assign the college an overall letter grade based on your evaluation of how well the college fits the criteria you established in **Worksheet 6**. Don't stress about this grade. It's simply a first impression based on your research.

Tips for Completing Worksheet 8

Where are you to find all this detailed information about schools? This section outlines a general approach to researching colleges, but your specific method will vary according to the resources available to you, the time you want to take to do this work, and the individual factors important to you in your college search.

As you begin your search, be wary of out-of-date or questionable sources of college information. Seek out people who know what is currently happening on a college campus. Don't rely on popular magazine articles listing the so-called "best" colleges; no completely objective criterion exists for rating colleges. Besides, only you and those who know you well can say what is best for you.

At this point, your goal is not to select the one college you feel best about. It is to begin to differentiate the colleges knowledgeably and narrow your list to those colleges where you will apply for admission.

You can use the tools mentioned earlier in this chapter to research each of the colleges you listed on **Worksheet 7**. Here are some additional resources for finding the information specified on the worksheet.

Review guidebooks and general college information websites. Begin with one or two of the following guidebooks: *Fiske Guide to Colleges, Colleges That Change Lives, Colleges That Create Futures, America's Best Colleges for B Students,* or *Princeton Review's Best Colleges.* In a few pages of narrative about each college as well as basic statistics (on location, size, etc.), these subjective guidebooks attempt to review the total environment of the college. They evaluate the quality of student life, the academic strengths and weaknesses, and the influence of the location on the nature of campus life. Even though you may be using one or more of these books as your initial way to check out colleges, remember that these types of reviews cannot speak for every student at each college; in fact, some students would disagree completely with the description of their own college. Indeed, experts on colleges also disagree— sometimes fervently—with certain descriptions. Student opinion websites are another way to expand your college knowledge. Some examples are colleges.niche.com, collegexpress.com, unigo.com, and collegeconfidential.com. As with any website offering opinions, remember that what one student dislikes about a college is exactly what another student loves.

If some of the colleges that you listed in **Worksheet 7** are not included in one of the subjective guidebooks—a very common occurrence, given that these books review fewer than 10% of colleges—consult one of the phonebook-sized guidebooks, such *Peterson's Four-Year Colleges* and *Barron's Profiles of American Colleges*, or comprehensive websites such as College Navigator (nces.ed.gov/collegenavigator/), collegedata.com, act.org, coplac.org, collegeboard.org, princetonreview.com, or usnews.com. These books and sites provide basic information about colleges as well as details on academic programs available, general requirements for admission, and cost of attendance. You might look at Princeton Review's Colleges That Pay You Back, which includes reviews of colleges that are not covered in many of the other guidebooks and also features a return on investment emphasis.

You can find a book on virtually any college topic from visiting campuses to essay writing to guidance on colleges from an ethnic/multicultural perspective. Check out **Appendix J, References for College Planning**, for a selection of titles.

Get information directly from the colleges. Find opportunities to talk with college representatives. College admission representatives visit high schools or conduct programs in various cities as a way to answer directly questions of prospective students. Here are some examples of the types of questions you may want to ask to further your research. What are the college's strongest departments? What role do fraternities/sororities play in the social life of the college? What financial aid options exist? Any issue important to you should be explored. Don't let fancy-sounding titles of the admission representatives scare you off— these college reps are there to answer your questions; your job is to ask the right ones.

You can also review printed or online material from the colleges. Colleges post tons of material on their websites and distribute information through their viewbooks and catalogues. If you would like specific information about some aspect such as the women's volleyball team, scholarships based on academic merit, or the program in pre-medicine, ask for it. Read through the material carefully. Keep in mind that colleges put their best foot forward, and naturally the materials they publish and post online are likely to be self-serving. Nonetheless, your systematic review of this information can be productive. As you read, ask yourself some of the following questions. What does each college emphasize about itself? What feeling do I get from reading the material or looking at the website? Does the college seem friendly, impersonal, spirited, stuffy, full of rules and requirements, diverse? Some colleges feature student blogs on their website, and these may offer a less-filtered view of the school.

Talk with people who attend or have attended the college. Recent graduates—and current students, provided they remain objective—can be a great source of inside information about a college, its academic offerings, and what life on campus is really like. If you know students or alumni of a school that interests you, ask them about their collegiate experience. Their perspective can be valuable, especially when they know you well. You may be able to obtain names by asking your high school counselor about graduates from your high school who currently attend or recently graduated from the colleges that interest you. You can also contact college admission offices for possible names of current students and alumni in your area. While talking to students and alumni can be helpful, remember, one, that schools change and, two, there are always a wide range of perceptions about the same school.

If you are on a formal campus tour or just visiting a campus, talk to the students you meet (and not just the tour guide) to find out what they like or dislike about their school. You can ask questions about their major, the effect of the school's location on the campus life, social opportunities, extracurricular activities, and anything else that matters to you.

Access websites of individual colleges and other organizations. You can access college websites easily. Some websites allow you to compare colleges on the basis of such criteria as college endowments, graduation rates, or other factors.

- Side-by-side comparison of different colleges (nces.ed.gov/ipeds) and fast facts and college data (nces.ed.gov/collegenavigator), both websites of the National Center for Education Statistics
- Compare colleges via College Scorecard, US Department of Education (collegescorecard.ed.gov)
- General rankings, including rankings from *US News & World Report* (usnews.com/best-colleges) and 50 Best Colleges for African Americans as rated by *Money* (https://money.com/best-colleges-african-americans/)
- Annual student survey of academic challenge, experiences with faculty, campus environment, and more from National Survey of Student Engagement (nsse.indiana.edu)
- Graduation rate by college from *The Chronicle of Higher Education* (collegecompletion.chronicle.com)
- General information, similar colleges, graduation rates and more at collegeresults.org
- College comparisons by tuition, graduation rates, etc. from the University and College Accountability Network (ucan-network.org)

One section on **Worksheet 8** asks you to comment on "life outside of class." Indeed, a key goal of researching is to find out what colleges are like, e.g., the type of students that attend, the level of academic pressure, and the general nature of social life. Knowing about student life on campus—including sports, campus issues, residence hall living, balance of study and socializing—is, in many ways, the most important research dimension. Yet digging up this information can be difficult because there are no scientific ways to accurately measure student or academic life. However, some of the methods described below may help you get a sense of college life at schools that interest you.

Look at the "student life" section of a college's website to see the clubs offered, the status of fraternities and sororities, the intramural sports opportunities, and so on. In addition, websites for particular college cities (the Chamber of Commerce site, for example) can tell you about the community in which the college is located. This information is particularly helpful for smaller, more isolated cities. Is there a symphony orchestra? Are there local rock clubs or theaters that attract a following? Are touring Broadway shows common? Does the city boast festivals or other activities (rodeos, car shows, food fairs) indigenous to the area? All of these can be helpful clues to student life.

Other websites also offer some glimpses of campus life through virtual campus tours, links to campus newspapers, and more. Some of these student life sites are a bit "off the wall." As for review sites, remember that reviews and statistics—whether for restaurants or universities— can be manipulated. So take details of review sites with a grain of salt, and bear in mind that anyone with a computer can comment on campus life. Here's a list of some popular sites and the information they provide.

- campusreel, campusreel.org/ (Campus Reel) (videos)
- campustours.com (virtual college and university tours)
- collegenews.com (information about college students and issues)
- colleges.niche.com (descriptions of colleges and reviews)
- collegexpress.com (general college information, listings, and more)
- greekpages.com (information on fraternity and sorority life)
- greekspot.com/collegenews (access to college newspapers)
- ncaa.org (information on athletics)
- newslink.org/statcamp.html (access to college newspapers)
- ratemyprofessors.com (rating of professors)
- studentsreview.com (student reviews of colleges)
- unigo.com (rankings, reviews, videos, photos, and more)
- usnews.com/best-colleges (rankings, college info, and statistics)
- youniversitytv.com (college and career-related videos)

Students can also call and/or e-mail various persons on college campuses. You might consider asking the admission office for the e-mail address of a student. Or, you can contact a residence hall or the student government or newspaper office by phone or e-mail. You could find the name of the president of a religious (or other interest) group. Ask the student questions about the college. You might start with, "I'm a high school student and I'm thinking about attending your school. I thought I'd learn about the college by talking to a few students." Yes, it is OK for students to do this. Colleges know that students who pick their school for the right reasons (and have their questions answered) are more likely to be successful once they are enrolled.

Obtain financial aid information. For financial aid and general money issues, students and parents might review the following websites that provide useful information.

- cappex.com (search on scholarships)
- salliemae.com/college-planning/ (Sallie Mae, a loan provider, addresses cost issues)
- collegeboard.org (search on financial aid and cost information)
- collegegold.com (costs calculator, scholarship search, financial planning)
- fafsa.ed.gov (complete the Free Application for Federal Financial Aid) though this link works, there is a new one at studentaid.gov/h/apply-for-aid/fafsa but there's no need to change what you have already
- https://studentaid.gov/h/apply-for-aid/fafsa (estimate of federal financial aid package, FAFSA4caster)
- fastweb.com (scholarship search, budgeting calculator)
- finaid.org (comprehensive financial aid information source)
- nasfaa.org (straight talk on financial aid, regional tuition discounts)

- savingforcollege.com (529 plan information, critiques, tools, and an excellent financial aid calculator)
- scholarships.com (scholarship search, resources)
- studentaid.ed.gov (types of aid, loan advice and management)
- financialaidtoolkit.ed.gov/tk/learn/fafsa/..(US Department of Education FAFSA information for counselors, but valuable information for all)

Filter information. Comparing colleges requires you to be a good researcher. Don't rely on one website, one book, or one person for information about colleges that interest you. This chapter lists lots of resources because multiple sources of information are better than just one. Always assess the reliability of the source, and check information from one source against another. Part of your research goal is to separate valid information from information that is old (colleges do change over time), untrue, distorted, prejudiced, or otherwise misguided.

Everyone seems to have an opinion about colleges, so don't be surprised if grandparents, distant cousins, neighbors, and even your mail carrier weigh in on your college search. You can listen to what they have to say; just remember that every person has an individual perspective. If Molly Jones from across the street didn't have a great experience at College A, try to find out why. The answer may be that College A was not right for Molly, who might have been looking for a different type of college than you are.

Make it personal. Talk to people, read a lot, and stay open to new information, but filter all information and always interpret it as it pertains to you and what you want in a college. No college is good or bad in the abstract. College A may have the perfect educational program, be the perfect size, be affordable, but its location is less than ideal for you. What do you do? You're not looking for the perfect college (remember, it probably doesn't exist). Rather, you're looking for a list of several colleges where you will be successful. So weigh the good points against the bad points and then, ultimately, decide whether that particular college belongs on your final college list.

Don't let stereotypes guide your choice of colleges. Small colleges are just as much fun as big colleges. More expensive colleges are not inherently "better." More "selective" colleges don't always provide a "better" education. Students in Maine get through winter without dog sleds (or even snowshoes). A degree from a "prestigious" college is not a prerequisite (nor a guarantee) for landing a high-paying job or getting into an excellent graduate school. And the list goes on. The important consideration remains, "Where will I fit in and be successful?"

Don't get frustrated by the volume of material available about each college. Make notes as you go. Don't just say, "All colleges sound the same." Look for differences.

Your impressions are the most important here. You are not looking for "good colleges." Rather, you are looking for good colleges for you. Keep in mind that even among your list of colleges (**Worksheet 7**), there may be features that do not appeal to you.

No doubt, through your research, you will learn some things about specific colleges that will cause you to stop considering them. For instance, at one school, you might find that fraternities and sororities play a much more significant role in the social scene than you realized or desired, and thus, cross that school off your list.

Worksheet 8—College Fact Finder

Name of College			
City and State Distance from a major city? How will I get there?			
Number of students enrolled?			
Does the college offer the academic programs (majors) I'm seeking? If undecided, what programs does the college offer that I'm interested in?			
Life outside of class: Does this college seem like an interesting place to be? What features (activities, traditions, location) pertaining to the student experience sound appealing?			
What is one positive feature about this college? One negative feature?			
Are my admission chances high, medium, or low? (See page 96 for guidelines.)			
What is the cost?			
Include tuition and room/board (if applicable).			
My notes about this college: Is there anything else I want to know about this school?			
On a grade scale from A to F, how would I rate this college as a match for me?			

Worksheet 8—College Fact Finder

Name of College			
City and State Distance from a major city? How will I get there?			
Number of students enrolled?			
Does the college offer the academic programs (majors) I'm seeking? If undecided, what programs does the college offer that I'm interested in?			
Life outside of class: Does this college seem like an interesting place to be? What features (activities, traditions, location) pertaining to the student experience sound appealing?			
What is one positive feature about this college? One negative feature?			
Are my admission chances high, medium, or low? (See page 96 for guidelines.)			
What is the cost?			
Include tuition and room/board (if applicable).			
My notes about this college: Is there anything else I want to know about this school?			
On a grade scale from A to F, how would I rate this college as a match for me?			

Worksheet 8—College Fact Finder

Name of College			
City and State Distance from a major city? How will I get there?			
Number of students enrolled?			
Does the college offer the academic programs (majors) I'm seeking? If undecided, what programs does the college offer that I'm interested in?			
Life outside of class: Does this college seem like an interesting place to be? What features (activities, traditions, location) pertaining to the student experience sound appealing?			
What is one positive feature about this college? One negative feature?			
Are my admission chances high, medium, or low? (See page 96 for guidelines.)			
What is the cost?			
Include tuition and room/board (if applicable).			
My notes about this college: Is there anything else I want to know about this school?			
On a grade scale from A to F, how would I rate this college as a match for me?			

Worksheet 8—College Fact Finder

Name of College			
City and State Distance from a major city? How will I get there?			
Number of students enrolled?			
Does the college offer the academic programs (majors) I'm seeking? If undecided, what programs does the college offer that I'm interested in?			
Life outside of class: Does this college seem like an interesting place to be? What features (activities, traditions, location) pertaining to the student experience sound appealing?			
What is one positive feature about this college? One negative feature?			
Are my admission chances high, medium, or low? (See page 96 for guidelines.)			
What is the cost?			
Include tuition and room/board (if applicable).			
My notes about this college: Is there anything else I want to know about this school?			
On a grade scale from A to F, how would I rate this college as a match for me?			

Guidelines for Determining Your Likelihood of Admission

As a part of your review of college options, you should consider your chances of admission. Look at the colleges still on your list and assign each to one of the three following categories:

Low chance of admission. These are colleges where your chance of admission is not likely, but still possible. Low-chance-of-admission colleges are sometimes called "reaches."

Medium chance of admission. At these colleges, your chance of admission is about 50/50. In other words, your chances seem just as good to be admitted as they are to be denied. You also put colleges in this category if you can't place them in either of the other categories.

High chance of admission. These are the colleges where you will likely be admitted. High-chance-of-admission colleges are often called "safeties" or "backups."

It is vital that you keep in mind that no foolproof method exists for separating colleges into these three groups. But ultimately, the goal is not precision, but good judgment. Talk with your counselor and ask for help with this task. Above all, be realistic about your assessment; rely on hard facts, not what you wish you had achieved.

1. Carefully consider your admission credentials. Think about the strength of your courses, GPA, test scores, extracurricular activities, and academic curiosity. How do you compare to others in your school in these areas? Be realistic. Ask teachers and counselors for input. Look at your answers on *Worksheet 4*.

2. Compare your GPA and test scores with those listed in the guidebooks for each of your colleges. Remember that you are judged on the basis of your success within your individual high school's grading system and on national metrics such as standardized test scores.

3. Look at the admission statistics, i.e., the percentage of students admitted. These statistics can be found in guidebooks such as the *Fiske Guide to Colleges* or on database sources such as collegedata.com and College Navigator, (nces.ed.gov/collegenavigator/). The following breakdown is only a guideline and can vary, depending your GPA, test scores (if submitted), your high school profile, etc.
    *   Colleges with an admission rate of 30% or lower may, depending on other factors described here, belong in the low-chance-of-admission category.
    *   Colleges with an admission rate of 31–75% may, depending on other factors described here, belong in the medium-chance-of-admission category. Because 31–75% is such a wide range, other admission factors described in this book should be looked at carefully.
    *   Colleges that admit more than 75% of students may, depending on other factors described here, belong in the high-chance-of-admission category.

4. Admission to colleges in the Ivy League and schools at that level of selectivity has become extremely competitive. The percentage of students admitted to the 50 most selective colleges is often n the single digits. As such I refer to admission at these colleges as "wild cards." It is nearly impossible to predict admission at these colleges and universities.

5. Some guidebooks (such as *Peterson's*, for example) list colleges according to such categories as "most difficult," "moderately difficult," etc. Your college list should include colleges from several of these categories.

There are other ways of evaluating your college choices on the basis of admission statistics. Look first at information from the college itself. For example, you can talk to college representatives who visit your high school or check the application statistics or profiles of admitted students that some colleges make available on their website. A profile for an admitted freshman class may provide such information as average GPA, percent of students receiving merit aid awards, and geographic distribution of first year students.

Another point that may be of interest is the history of student acceptances from your high school. Ask your counselor for information on grade point averages or test scores of students from your school who applied and were accepted at your colleges of interest.

As you do your evaluating, be optimistic as well as realistic. Your "odds" of admission are based on your record and background, the level of the competition for places in the freshman class, and other factors. Although comparing yourself against data mined from guidebooks is a first step, you will learn in **Chapter 8** that admission officers take many factors into account to determine your "acceptability." Lower test scores, for example, can be offset by strong college preparatory courses. In addition, your grade point average, extracurricular involvements, level of curiosity, and other qualities may suggest a greater or lesser chance of admission. Discuss any admission issues and questions with your college advisor. He or she will use knowledge based on experience with many other students to help you make these judgments.

Deciding Where to Apply

After you have completed **Worksheet 8, College Fact Finder**, go back and analyze your research for each of your colleges. Sort through your Fact Finders. Look at the notes you made for each school. In addition to the overall grade given, look at high and low points for each college. From this analysis, you should have some colleges you like a lot and some that don't quite measure up.

Through this process of elimination, you will be able to refine and reduce your initial list of colleges and move to **Worksheet 9, Your Apply List.** Congratulations! This is a great step forward.

Worksheet 9 has spaces for ten colleges, but the number of colleges you apply to will depend on several factors. Students today apply to more colleges than they did a few years ago, but more than ten may mean that you have not done your research.

This is a good time to discuss your list with your counselor and your parents. This list reflects your best thinking about those colleges that, based on your research and the "feel" you get from them, seem to be places where you would be happy and successful.

Final Considerations

As you work on completing **Worksheet 9** and finalizing your apply list, consider the four questions that follow. Your answers will help in determining whether you need to expand or shrink your apply list.

1. Are colleges included on your list because they fit on the basis of your reading and your general analysis? Your colleges should be more than just "names." Keep in mind that college planning is not about getting into a top school—it is, more importantly, about fitting in and being happy.

2. Does your list of schools represent a good match of your interests and talents, as well as the strengths of the colleges?

3. Do you have some appealing high-chance-of-admission ("backup") colleges? Having solid backups is important, especially in these days of increased college selectivity. As mentioned above, some colleges these days are accepting a tiny fraction of those who apply. Some students spend a great deal of time deciding on their low chance ("reach") colleges and relatively little time choosing their backups. Your backups are essential to good college planning. You are looking for a balance in terms of admission selectivity. If you apply to eight colleges, for example, you should have one or two schools that are "low chance" of admission, two or three that are "medium chance" of admission, and two or three that are "high chance" of admission. And regardless of selectivity, each and every school on your list should be one that you would be happy to attend.

4. Do you have a financial safety school? This is the college (perhaps a local state university) where cost is agreeable with your parents.

If the answer to any of these questions is "no," you should rethink your college selection criteria and talk with your advisors. If the answers are "yes," congratulations! You are on the road to a good college choice.

Worksheet 9—Your Apply List

Name of College	Location
1.	
2.	
3.	
4.	
5.	
6.	
7.	
8.	
9.	
10.	

Application Completion: Keeping on Track

Worksheet 10, Application Timetable, is designed to help you get organized and monitor the numerous deadlines associated with applying to college.

Step 1. Complete the left column with the name of each college from **Worksheet 9**. If you are applying to more than ten colleges, make a copy of the timetable. Read the application materials for each college thoroughly so you can become more familiar with procedures applicable to each of your college choices. In addition, find out how your school processes applications. Some high schools use organizing web portals such as Naviance, MAIA, Scoir, and Cialfo. What are your responsibilities? Is your high school responsible for mailing your transcript and/or your application? If you apply online, how will your transcript and teacher recommendations be sent? Are completed teacher recommendations given to you, sent directly to the college, or handed over to the counseling office? You should also find out how much lead time your high school office needs for sending out transcripts and applications.

Step 2. Fill in the Level of Admission Difficulty column by determining, to the best of your ability, the level of selectivity for each of your college choices. Is the college a low chance of admission school (a "reach"), a high chance of admission (a "backup"), or a medium chance of admission for you? (Refer back to the section **Guidelines for Determining your Likelihood of Admission** on page 96 for guidance on making this assessment.)

Step 3. In the next column, Application Method, note how you intend to apply to each college. Most colleges allow you to submit either a paper or online application, and usually you can apply electronically from the college's own website. More than 900 colleges accept the Common Application (commonapp.org), about a hundred accept the Coalition for Access, Affordability, and Success Application (coalitionforcollegeaccess.org), and several dozen accept the Universal Application (universalcollegeapp.com). The Common Black College Application (commonblackcollegeapp.com) is also available. If you are using the Common Application, you should also check to see if the college requests any supplementary material. Do you have an application or know how to access one? If not, go to the perspective student/ admission section of the college website and complete an information request form, e-mail, or call to receive an application.

Step 4. Record the deadline for submission of the application for each college.

Step 5. Once you know when the application is due, establish your own target date for submitting your application. This will keep you organized and moving forward during the fall of your senior year. Look at the application deadlines; your target date should be well in advance of the deadline set by the college in order to give yourself time to complete the application and the essays in an unhurried way. Many students try to complete all of their applications by Thanksgiving of their senior year; others try to have them in the mail by the start of winter vacation.

Step 6. In the next column, record information about your essays. Most colleges ask students to write an essay. Some require only one, while a few very selective schools require one or two major essays, as well as a number of shorter responses. Be sure to list all of the writing tasks required—essays, personal statements, short answers, and brief paragraphs. With this list, you can tell which assignments are most common and whether there are any overlapping topics (in other words, essays you can adapt for more than one college). From here, you can systematically begin writing. Start work on your essays well before the application due date to give yourself time to refine and polish your writing. You'll find essay strategies in **Chapter 7.**

Step 7. In the next column, list the standardized tests the colleges accept for admission and/ or indicate the date scores were sent. If you are submitting scores, you notify the testing agency (College Board or ACT) to send your scores directly to your colleges.

Step 8. The next column deals with recommendations. A recommendation from your high school counselor is commonly required. In addition, many colleges ask for teacher recommendations. For each of your colleges, check to see what recommendations are required. Do you need to meet with your counselor in order for him/her to prepare a recommendation for you? Have you asked your teachers? How are the recommendations transmitted to the college?

Step 9. The next column allows you to insert the date that your high school transcript was sent to the college.

Step 10. The remaining column—labeled "Other"—allows you to personalize the Application Timetable. What other documents are needed? You may, for example, use this column to track required financial aid forms (and deadlines) or to indicate the date of your music audition or contacts with a coach. This may also be the place to note the deadline for applying for on-campus housing. Record how you are going to use the column in the blank spaces at the top of the Application Timetable.

Keeping track of all this information allows you to stay focused during a busy time in your life. Taking just a few minutes each week to see where you are, allowing time to complete essays, etc., will make a big difference in your level of sanity during your senior year.

Worksheet 10—Application Timetable

College/University	Level of Admission Difficulty	Application Method	College Application Deadline	My Target Application Submission Date
1.				
2.				
3.				
4.				
5.				
6.				
7.				
8.				
9.				
10.				

Worksheet 10—Application Timetable

Essay Information	Standardized Testing Scores (if submitted)	Teacher Recommendations	Transcript Sent?	Other

Now that you have identified and compared colleges, the next chapter focuses on an important way to learn about a college: the campus visit.

Chapter 6
Learning From Campus Visits

The process of making a good college choice involves several important steps. By considering your goals, your interests, and your achievements, you have begun the process of considering colleges and comparing them with your requirements and ideals.

Common Questions about Campus Visits

Chapter 5 presented an array of resources available to help you make a good college choice. Your parents, college advisors, and a variety of material in print and on the web will give you a sense of the life at a particular college. But one important way for you to find out whether you might feel comfortable on a campus is to visit the college itself and observe your own reactions to the campus, the people, and the general atmosphere of the college. This chapter answers the questions most commonly asked about campus visits.

1. "Why should I visit colleges?"

The best reason for visiting is to learn about the college first-hand. Usually students return from their college visits with new impressions and perspectives about places they previously knew only from websites, written material, or the comments of others. Campus visits bring colleges to life, and they're an excellent way for you to find out if the college would be a good place for you to live for four years. You visit to learn more and to expand the fact-finding process. While few colleges still require on-campus interviews (and seldom will such meetings be the critical factor in a decision on your application), visits do show your interest in the school. In sum, visitation can be very helpful in your college shopping.

You should also visit to go beyond the stereotypes and generalizations often found in our society, particularly on social media. Visits give you the chance to make your own conclusions about the worth of a particular college for you.

If cost and/or time are issues, use other resources to find out about your potential college choices—at least in the initial phases of your investigation. Consult the sources of college information mentioned in the previous chapter.

2. "How should I prepare for campus visits?"

Obviously, first you must decide which colleges you will visit. While you may have neither time nor resources to visit all of the colleges your counselor recommends, neither should you visit only those that are the most competitive for you. In general, you should plan campus visits to four or five schools that represent different levels of competitiveness and choice for you. *Chapter 5* discussed ways to think about your chances of admission. Ideally, you would visit your first- or second-choice schools only after visiting others further down your list. You will profit from the experience and the perspective you gain with every visit to a campus, and will have a better sense of what to ask and look for at the next school you look at.

3. "When should I visit colleges?"

The optimum time to visit colleges will vary for each student. If you have planned well ahead and have identified colleges appropriate for you, the spring of your junior year is a good time to see campuses. Very long-term planners might visit in the spring of the sophomore year.

Many students visit campuses during the summer between their junior and senior years. Although this is not the best time to see a campus "in action" (since students who may be on campus at that time may not be representative of those who attend between September and June), summer is a relaxed time for admission personnel, who may be more available to answer questions. In addition, because summer is often the easiest time for families to get away, many families tour colleges together, combining these visits with their vacations. (This also provides an opportunity for younger sibling to get a sense of a college environment and think about their own college prospects.) But be careful that summer visits to your prospective colleges don't become "architectural tours," where you stroll around admiring the beauty of the buildings and campus greenery. Attend any information sessions that are available, and make an effort to talk with students and faculty who may be available. Campus beauty and weather conditions are secondary to your fit with the college.

The fall or winter of your senior year is a good time to see the campus, and at some schools, the best time to meet someone from the admission office. Selective colleges may fill their appointment schedule early, so the key advice for visiting highly selective college campuses is to call early to make an appointment.

The spring of your senior year, after you have received all your admission decisions, is a good time to visit and make your final choice. Some colleges have days set aside for admitted students to visit. Be aware that admission offices can be quite hectic at this time of year and making travel arrangements without much advanced planning may be expensive.

If you participate in a sport, and you want to continue that sport while attending college, you may want to visit campuses while your sport is in season.

Your other decision is what day of the week to visit. To gain a real sense of campus life—meet some students, sit in on classes, and participate in some typical activities—you should schedule your visits during weekdays of the regular school year. Although some admission offices are open on Saturday mornings, most campuses are fairly quiet on weekends. Also, to get a good sense of a campus and its people, you want to visit on a "normal" day, so avoid exam weeks and big football game weekends. You can check a school's academic calendar on the college website to find out exam schedules and dates of fall and spring breaks or other vacation days.

No matter when you schedule your campus visits, remember that these visits will be most beneficial if they occur after you have discussed college options with your parents and counselor and conducted your own research on recommended colleges (and completed **Worksheet 8** in **Chapter 5**). Save your time (and your parents' money) to visit campuses that match the qualities you want in a school.

4. "I am visiting several colleges in one trip. How much time should I spend on each campus?"

Try to spend as much time as possible at each college. Most students need at least half a day for each visit; a visit of less than three hours is insufficient to gain a good sense of a college. An overnight stay is ideal. If you have friends currently enrolled at a school you plan to visit, ask about the possibility of staying with one of them. You may have to sleep on the floor, but it will be worth the inconvenience to gain a close-up look at the college.

5. "What arrangements need to be made before I visit?"

Arrange for your visit by contacting the admission office at each school you plan to visit. You should call or e-mail several weeks in advance of your desired visit date. As mentioned previously, the most selective colleges fill up interview times several months ahead, although it is still possible to have a campus tour or an information session. (Information sessions are addressed in detail in Question 10.)

If you do not stay on the campus, ask the admission office for recommendations about motels or hotels nearby. Schedule your appointments so you arrive in plenty of time. Study maps and transportation schedules; allow extra time to find a college if you are unfamiliar with the region or city in which it is located.

Many colleges and universities have a set routine that involves a campus tour and may include a meeting with someone from the admission office or a general information session (see Question 10). These days, "meetings" with admission officers at colleges are rarely "interviews" in the formal sense but more often are non-evaluative discussions or talks; see Question 8 for more information.

At some colleges, you may be able to make arrangements with the admission office to personalize your visit—take a tour, meet with a member of the admission staff, attend a class, meet with a professor, and eat in a dining hall—and staff will make the necessary arrangements. At other schools, you will be asked to make calls to other offices to arrange features of your visit. Some students meet with a coach, others want to see the studio art facilities. Your visit should be shaped by your interests.

If possible, spend a night in a campus residence hall. If you know students on the campus, call them and ask if you can be their guest for a night or if they have time to spend with you when you visit.

Whatever you do, talk to as many students as you can during your visit. In addition, pay attention to bulletin boards and the campus newspaper; both are good guides to campus activities. See the list of "do's and don'ts" later in this chapter.

The website travelmath.com can help you plan your trip. It allows you to quickly access driving time, closest airport, and major cities nearby.

6. "What sort of questions should I ask?"

Given that the purpose of your college visits is to research your level of comfort at the schools, your questions should try to get at the heart of what the school is really like. Some questions may be general and apply to every school you visit; others may be more specific. You will gain the most insight into the colleges you tour if your questions go beyond the obvious, i.e., the ones answered in the viewbook or other publications or on college websites. Ask about those issues and topics that matter to you. Don't hesitate to ask the nitty-gritty questions.

To arrive at the key questions that are important to you, review the characteristics of your ideal college, **Worksheet 6**. A few general questions are listed here.

The following questions can be asked of students, college admission officers, or faculty. (You may get surprisingly different answers to some of these, depending on whom you ask.)

- Why do students select this college?
- What is the best thing about your college?
- What is the glue that binds social life? Is it the outdoors? Fraternities and sororities? Athletics? Intellectual discussions?
- What do students complain about most?
- Describe the sorts of students who thrive here and the kinds of students who are less successful/satisfied in this environment.
- How active is the social life?
- What type of student seems happiest at your college?
- What are the most popular majors?
- What are the most popular extracurricular activities?
- What are the opportunities for extracurricular participation?
- What are student traditions? (Some examples include guys wearing coats and ties to football games, a free day in the fall to play in the mountains, a historic athletic rivalry).
- How active is the college in helping students with career planning?
- What happens here on weekends? Do students stay on campus?
- How safe is your campus? How comfortable will I feel walking through your campus alone at night?
- Do students know one or two professors well enough to ask them for a work or a graduate school recommendation? These recommendations are often an important part of career advancement and admission to graduate or professional school.
- How good is the faculty advising for selecting classes and fulfilling requirements?

The following questions are geared toward students you may meet.

- Has the college lived up to your expectations?
- How does your impression of the campus compare to the description in one of the guidebooks (The Fiske Guide, for example)?
- How does your impression of the campus compare to what you had heard from your college counselor or independent educational consultant?
- Is there anything in particular I should see during my time on campus?
- What do faculty members expect of students?
- When did you last meet individually with a professor?
- How much time does a typical student spend on homework each week?
- How much reading and writing are expected from students in most classes?
- How often is material that is learned in class discussed outside class?
- How electronic is the campus? Are syllabi or other resources available online? Can papers be submitted electronically?
- Does the college have an organized program to assist students who need help getting a higher grade in a class?
- How would you evaluate the balance between time devoted to academics and time spent on personal matters and social activities?
- Would you describe the academic feeling among students as competitive or cooperative?
- Would you characterize the student body politically as mostly conservative, liberal, or moderate?
- Are many students involved in regular volunteer work?
- What does a typical day look like?
- Tell me about campus life. Is it dominated by frat parties? House parties? Small parties? The bar scene?
- How are roommates chosen?
- Are there noise-free or substance-free residence halls?
- How laid-back are the dining halls? Can I wear pajamas to breakfast? Are shoes required?
- Is it safe to leave a backpack or a laptop in the library while I grab a cup of coffee?

The following questions can be directed toward admission officers or professors.

- What are typical course requirements, e.g., how many exams, papers, etc.?
- Who teaches introductory courses—professors or graduate students?
- What departments are considered outstanding, weak, and average?
- Why is this a good college for me to study my selected major?
- What if I am unsure about my major? What kind of feedback do students receive on coursework and how often do they get it? Is this a good place for me to learn more about different fields?
- Will any of my high school courses (honors level, AP, IB, for example) count for college credit?

- What constitutes a typical freshman-year program?
- How much freedom do I have in selecting freshman courses?
- What percentage of freshman courses are required (versus elective)?
- How many elective classes can I take over my four years?
- What arrangements are made for advising and tutorial help?
- What percentage of students study abroad?
- Are internships or independent study opportunities common?
- After graduation, what do students do? Go to grad school? Get a job?

Having asked these questions and others, your campus visits will be most beneficial if you use **Worksheet 11, Campus Visit Notes**, to jot down your finding and impressions about each college.

7. "Should my parents accompany me on campus visits?"

Parents can be great for helping you determine your level of comfort and your ability to succeed at a given college. Also, parents often have questions of their own. And they do have an investment—financial and otherwise—in your plans for the future.

But while parents can be helpful and supportive throughout the visit, they should not participate in the personal meeting with admission officers. While you are involved in an admission meeting, your parents may want to schedule a visit with a financial aid officer or just walk around the campus. Following your visit, share your reactions and observations with your parents before asking for their impressions. Then weigh their comments with yours as you think about each college.

8. "What is a personal interview on campus and how important is it?"

An interview is most often a general discussion with the student about past educational attainment, interests, and motivation toward college. The personal interview is rarely a required part of the admission process and is seldom a deciding factor in accepting or rejecting a candidate. An interview does not transform an unacceptable applicant into an acceptable one.

An interview can, however, be an excellent way to learn about a college. It is a two-way exchange. You should be ready to ask questions that will help you learn more about the college and be prepared to answer questions that will help the interviewer learn more about you. Here are some typical questions and requests you may encounter during the interview.

- Tell me something about yourself as a student.
- How did you become interested in this college?
- What things are most important to you as you compare colleges?
- What are your interests, strengths, and weaknesses?
- Do you have any questions? (This is usually asked, so be ready!)

Before the interview begins, you should have identified one or two things about yourself that you want the interviewer to be aware of. Be sure to mention them when the interviewer says, "Is there anything else we should know about you?"

In addition, don't hesitate to share the leadership of the conversation. You are not on the witness stand or being grilled by the authorities. Use your time with an admission officer to obtain information to help you determine whether the college is a good match for you. Remember that colleges want to make both your campus visit and your interview a positive experience.

In addition to personal interviews on campus, many selective colleges may arrange interviews with alumni who live near your city or town. These interviews are helpful because alums can be valuable sources of information about a college. Remember, however, that these individuals are likely to be volunteers (not employees of the university), and as such, their level of up-to-date information about the college may vary considerably.

9. "What are some tips for a meeting with an admission representative?"

- Dress comfortably. Wear regular school clothing.
- Be honest and be yourself. Don't try to second-guess yourself or tell the interviewer what you think he or she wants to hear.
- Ask questions.
- Make eye contact.
- Make a note of the person's name.
- Try to find out where you stand. If you feel comfortable and the meeting seems to be drawing to a close, you might ask about your admission chances based on the information you've shared.

10. "What are information sessions?"

If you don't want a personal meeting or if the college doesn't offer them, ask if the school provides a group information session. At these sessions, an admission officer speaks to a group of prospective students and parents and then often addresses their individual questions. Group size can range from fewer than a dozen attendees to fifty or more.

11. "Do colleges ever have special days when prospective students can visit?"

Yes, many colleges schedule special visitation days for prospective students. During a college-day program, a school often focuses all its resources on the needs of visitors. If you enjoy being around other students and like to participate as a member of a group, the college visit program will be an exciting experience. If you want more personalized attention, you should try to schedule an individual visit.

12. "What should I do after I visit a campus?"

Send a thank-you note to those who were helpful on your visit. (You remembered—of course!—to jot down the names of the individuals you met.) Writing a note of thanks is a gracious and polite response to those who assisted you. If you met with an admission officer, try to mention something specific and/or memorable about the encounter that impressed you; this will help the interviewer remember you.

13. "What other resources can I use for my campus visits?"

The US College and University Reference Map (hedbergmaps.com) is a great visual aid for learning about locations of colleges (and their proximity to each other) and for planning travel to college campuses.

14. "My family's funds are limited. We can't afford a tour of colleges. How can I learn about colleges?"

If you can't travel hundreds or thousands of miles to learn about colleges, try to visit a few colleges in your state. Choose nearby private, small liberal arts colleges as well as medium or large state universities. These visits will help you get the feel of different types of institutions. If time and funds allow, you can visit the schools to which you have been admitted later.

Attend any campus visit programs sponsored by colleges near you. Sit in on a class and, most importantly, talk with students. If you have friends who are currently enrolled in college, quiz them about their experiences when they are home on vacation or communicate with them electronically. Attend any college night programs held at your high school. See if you can meet with local alumni of schools that are on your list. You can even telephone or e-mail the admission office and request that a student be in touch with you to talk about the college. And finally, look back at some of the resources from *Chapter 5* that you used to build your college list; some of these tools can be used to explore your college options.

15. "How do I tell whether a college is a good match for me?"

View your campus visit as one important way to assess a college, but not as the only way. In completing the various worksheets to create your list of colleges where you will apply, you defined the characteristics of your ideal college. Everything you learn from a campus visit should be measured against the qualities you listed as important on *Worksheet 6* in *Chapter 3*.

Campus Visits: Some Final Do's and Don'ts

- Do consider visiting alone (especially colleges close to your home) so that you can decide how well the school fits your needs.
- Do visit with your parents to gain another perspective (and a free meal on the night of your visit).
- Do talk to students on every campus.
- Do follow up your visit with a thank-you note.
- Do analyze the whole school.
- Do take photographs.
- Do read copies of the student newspaper.
- Do look at the bulletin boards and other postings. What's happening on campus? Do these activities interest you?
- Do roam the campus by yourself. Look for clues that the college is a place where you would fit in.
- Do walk or drive around the community surrounding the college.
- Do go to the student activities office. What clubs are most popular? Are first-year students able to get involved in most organizations? Does one type of activity—sports, Greek letter organizations, the local bar scene—seem to dominate?
- Do check out the public transportation system.
- Do consider the ease of getting to and from the campus. If air travel is involved, are there direct flights?
- Do consider whether the school seems like a place where you can picture yourself spending the next four years.
- Do judge schools after you return home and have time to think over all of your visits.
- Don't evaluate the school on the basis of a visit with one student.
- Don't make snap judgments.
- Don't judge a college solely on your impressions of the tour guide.
- Don't let the weather on the day of your visit influence your impression.
- Don't let perceived quality or academic reputation totally affect you. Your task is to find the right colleges for you.
- Don't judge the college solely on impressions made on your visit. Remember what you have read and heard about the college before you set foot on the campus.
- Don't stand out. Try to blend in for the full college experience of what life is like on the campus.

And one final tip: Do record your observations. The best way to remember your impressions of each college is to write them down. Otherwise, you are apt to forget which school had the great dorms and which humanities program seemed perfect for you. **Worksheet 11, Campus Visit Notes,** provides space for you to record your impressions of four colleges. Make a copy of the worksheet for each additional campus you visit.

Worksheet 11—Campus Visit Notes

Name of College:

Location: _____

Date of Visit: _____

Names of people I spoke to: _____

Campus Facilities

My comments about the campus, residential halls, and other facilities. Was there anything I especially liked or disliked?

_____

_____

_____

_____

_____

_____

Student Life

My comments about student life on campus. From what I observed, is there a good chance I could fit in with the students here? Why or why not?

_____

_____

_____

_____

_____

_____

Academic Factors

My comments about academics. Does this college seem like the right place for me to study and learn? Why or why not?

_____

_____

_____

_____

_____

_____

Overall Impressions

What did I like best? What did I like least?

_____

_____

_____

_____

_____

_____

Other facts I want to remember about this college:

_____

_____

_____

_____

_____

_____

My Overall Assessment of How Well This College Fits Me:

Not Very Well	1	2	3	4	5	Extremely Well

Worksheet 11—Campus Visit Notes

Name of College:

Location: _____

Date of Visit: _____

Names of people I spoke to: _____

Campus Facilities

My comments about the campus, residential halls, and other facilities. Was there anything I especially liked or disliked?

_____

_____

_____

_____

_____

_____

Student Life

My comments about student life on campus. From what I observed, is there a good chance I could fit in with the students here? Why or why not?

_____

_____

_____

_____

_____

_____

Academic Factors

My comments about academics. Does this college seem like the right place for me to study and learn? Why or why not?

_____

_____

_____

_____

_____

_____

Overall Impressions

What did I like best? What did I like least?

_____

_____

_____

_____

_____

_____

Other facts I want to remember about this college:

_____

_____

_____

_____

_____

_____

My Overall Assessment of How Well This College Fits Me:

Not Very Well	1	2	3	4	5	Extremely Well

Worksheet 11—Campus Visit Notes

Name of College:

Location: _____

Date of Visit: _____

Names of people I spoke to: _____ ._____

Campus Facilities

My comments about the campus, residential halls, and other facilities. Was there anything I especially liked or disliked?

_____

_____

_____

_____

_____

_____

Student Life

My comments about student life on campus. From what I observed, is there a good chance I could fit in with the students here? Why or why not?

_____

_____

_____

_____

_____

_____

Academic Factors

My comments about academics. Does this college seem like the right place for me to study and learn? Why or why not?

_____

_____

_____

_____

_____

_____

Overall Impressions

What did I like best? What did I like least?

_____

_____

_____

_____

_____

_____

Other facts I want to remember about this college:

_____

_____

_____

_____

_____

_____

My Overall Assessment of How Well This College Fits Me:

Not Very Well	1	2	3	4	5	Extremely Well

Worksheet 11—Campus Visit Notes

Name of College:

Location: _____

Date of Visit: _____

Names of people I spoke to: _____

Campus Facilities

My comments about the campus, residential halls, and other facilities. Was there anything I especially liked or disliked?

_____

_____

_____

_____

_____

_____

Student Life

My comments about student life on campus. From what I observed, is there a good chance I could fit in with the students here? Why or why not?

_____

_____

_____

_____

_____

_____

Academic Factors

My comments about academics. Does this college seem like the right place for me to study and learn? Why or why not?

_____

_____

_____

_____

_____

Overall Impressions

What did I like best? What did I like least?

_____

_____

_____

_____

_____

_____

Other facts I want to remember about this college:

_____

_____

_____

_____

_____

My Overall Assessment of How Well This College Fits Me:

Not Very Well	1	2	3	4	5	Extremely Well

Chapter 7

Making Your Essays Work For You

At this point, you have already made some important decisions about the colleges you will consider as well as the colleges to which you will apply. Now you are ready to begin the process of preparing your college essay. The essay—more accurately called a "personal statement" since it varies from a traditional essay written for a school assignment—is usually the most time-consuming part of the application, and it deserves the most attention.

This chapter is divided into three sections. **Worksheet 12, Tackling Sample Essay Questions**, explains the reasoning behind the essay prompts commonly found on applications and assists you in thinking through your answers. **Worksheet 13, Essay**

Brainstorming, takes you through a process to generate additional essay ideas. The final section features specific hints for writing excellent and highly communicative essays.

While there are snippets, this chapter does not include full essays used by students in their own college applications. Reading these kinds of samples may impair your own creativity and constrain your thinking, leading you to write pale imitations. No essays are generically "good" or "bad" or "right" or "wrong." There are only good or bad essays for you. Everyone has his or her own special qualities and stories to tell. And those stories are the substance of good essays.

Before You Start

In case you are wondering, colleges really do read your essays. True, a few large universities rely primarily on grade point averages and maybe test scores to make admission decisions, but the vast majority of admission committees actually read, study, and ponder carefully the words you write on your essays. In fact, at some colleges, your application will be read by two, three, or more people. Moreover, your application may be discussed at length by a group of admission people in a committee meeting. Therefore the application essay should communicate what you would like a group of strangers to know about you. Many students are not accustomed to using a written description as a key way of communicating images of themselves, and this can make college applications and essays difficult for them.

Perhaps the most formidable barrier to essay writing is a lack of confidence about writing in general and personal writing in specific. Many students start the process by wondering what colleges want to see in an essay. This type of thinking is a waste of time! Don't try to "psyche out" an admission committee by deciding what it wants to read. Rather, the most important question you can ask yourself is: What is it about me that I want colleges to know? Colleges are interested in knowing about you, your interests, your feelings, your reactions, your insights, your qualities, your passions, your satisfactions, and your disappointments. The extent to which you tell your own meaningful story in an interesting, readable, and articulate way is the extent to which your essay is good.

No easy, quick solution is offered here for building writing confidence. But often students are surprised to find that the incident or reaction they thought most unsuitable for a college essay is exactly the one that is most important and revealing about them. Do not try to be anyone else in your essay. Tell about yourself and you'll write a solid, meaningful essay. And no matter how terrific your parents think you are, resist the urge to share their appraisal with the admissions committee. Your essay should not seem as if you are patting yourself on the back—save that for someone else!

In their applications, colleges ask a variety of essay questions. Some questions are specific ("Tell us how a book you read in the last year has influenced you"), and others are very broad and general ("Tell us something about yourself that will help us get to know you better"). Keep in mind that some essay questions may be similar among college-specific applications, or that colleges may share identical questions if they use generic applications such as the Common Application (commonapp.org), the Coalition Application (coalitionforcollegeaccess.org), the Common Black College Application (commonblackcollegeapp.com) or the Universal Application (universalcollegeapp.com). Many colleges call the essay a personal statement, some make the essay optional, and some require no essay at all. With few exceptions, though, most students gain by enclosing a personal statement with their application (even when it is not required).

There are websites and books devoted to helping with college essays. Some are listed in "The Application Process" section of **Appendix J, References for College Planning**. The older National Public Radio (NPR) series "This I Believe" provides a framework many students find helpful in finding the right "voice" for an essay. These essays are available in book form and via the NPR website.

Worksheet 12 lists common essay questions with a series of brainstorming strategies for each. By brainstorming, you'll arrive at one or two ideas you can use in preparing your very own answer to the question. After you complete **Worksheet 12**, move right on to **Worksheet 13**. Your answers to these open-ended questions may suggest other topics to consider as you begin working on your applications. These two worksheets should give you a good head start on your essay writing.

After you finish this chapter and after you identify your college choices, make a list of all the essays, personal statements, or other writing assignments your colleges require. Then, prioritize your writing requirements on the basis of application deadlines and your own target dates, as listed in **Chapter 5, Worksheet 10**.

Worksheet 12—Tackling Sample Essay Questions

Topic 1—Why have you selected University of the Brainiacs? Or, what would you bring to the diversity of our college community?

Some colleges may ask why you chose to apply to their particular institution. For this essay, list the qualities that led you to choose that particular college. You might also indicate other factors that promoted your interest. This is a point where all your careful self-assessment and research will come into good use. Review the factors you listed as important in selecting a college, specifically **Worksheet 6** in **Chapter 3**.

If you are applying to the fictitious University of the Brainiacs (UOB), compare these factors on your list to the distinguishing features of the UOB. You should find that many features at UOB fit the criteria you feel are important in your college choice. For example, UOB may be perfect because you were seeking a small liberal arts college with friendly students located in a rural area. Perhaps you visited UOB or talked to its representative. Or you may have been impressed with what an alumna said about UOB. All these are valid reasons why you feel UOB is a good choice.

As for adding to the diversity of the college community, consider, as you did with other topics, the person you are and the life experiences you've had. One can add to diversity through ideas, cultural/religious/ethnic heritage, interests, perspectives on the world, and so on.

Now choose one of your current favorite colleges and either describe why you would like to attend or detail what you would bring to the diversity of the campus community:

_____

_____

_____

_____

_____

_____

_____

Topic 2—Evaluate a significant experience, achievement, risk you have taken, or ethical dilemma you have faced and its impact on you.

Of all the questions asked by colleges, this is perhaps the most common. It provides you with an amazing number of opportunities to write about those aspects of your life that are most important to you.

The word "significant" in this question is critical because it requires personal reflection; an experience becomes significant when it causes us to see ourselves or others in a new or different way. In other words, just because you've never weathered a typhoon or won a national ski racing championship doesn't mean you lack "significant" experiences. Even at seventeen, you've had experiences that have affected you deeply and that others will find interesting. For example, one student produced a very thoughtful essay about the changes that occurred at home when her mom decided to go to college full-time. Another student wrote about the significance of visiting his grandmother every summer on a farm in Nebraska. Still another student received a traffic ticket and wrote about how he reacted to and what he learned from his encounter with the law. One young man used his essay to paint a word portrait of the expanded family he gained when his mother remarried.

As you reflect on possible topics, remember that an experience that affects you has no prescribed length. An important experience may last several minutes, several hours, days, or months. The most important consideration is that the experience had a memorable impact on you. In this essay, you will describe the experience and how you felt about it and discuss what it reveals about you.

The same considerations apply if you consider a risk you took or an ethical dilemma you faced or a challenge you overcame. In every case, it's important that your essay reveals an element of your personality. The risk or dilemma or challenge is less important than what you learned or how you changed. Remember that conflicting feelings and uncertainty can provide the material for a good essay.

Try this: Close your eyes, and for a few minutes think about everything that's happened to you since you became a high school freshman. No doubt a few of those memories are a bit more vivid, a bit clearer than others. Usually, those vivid memories represent "significant" experiences.

Now that they're fresh in your mind, briefly list a few of your significant experiences:

_____

_____

_____

_____

_____

_____

Excellent! Now, in a few phrases, explain why one of those experiences was significant. What did you learn about yourself as the result of the experience? Here's how one student began:

> *My younger brother's struggle with a severe hearing loss has affected me significantly because I have had to grow up rapidly and assume some added responsibilities at home. Sometimes it's real scary, because I don't exactly know how to do the things I am expected to do in taking care of him.*

It's your turn below:

_____

_____

_____

_____

_____

_____

_____

You now have the beginnings of the essay about a significant experience. If the question directs you to write about a significant achievement or accomplishment, you will follow a similar process, reviewing your achievement or accomplishment and describing its effect on you.

Topic 3—Briefly elaborate on one of your extracurricular activities or work experiences.

This question is relatively easy. Think about everything you do to occupy your time when you are not in school or studying. Refer to your ***Activities/ Experiences Record***, ***Worksheet 3***. Do you play the piano, sew your own clothes, play sports, or write articles for the school paper? Do you work, take care of a younger sibling, or volunteer at a nursing home? The key here is identifying an activity that has meaning for you. ***First, list the meaningful activity:***

_____

_____

_____

Now consider the ways in which the activity has been meaningful for you. As you think, go beyond the obvious. It is normal, for instance, that a team sport like soccer might be meaningful because you learned teamwork. But no doubt you also learned a great deal more than teamwork by playing soccer. Did you learn how to deal with disappointment? Did you learn that "people skills" are not as easy as you thought? This is one student's thesis about her experiences as a field hockey player:

> *Playing field hockey last year was significant for me. I learned that I am not as good a leader as I am a follower, and for the first time, I learned how to deal with people I don't like.*

Now, write a sentence or two that tells, specifically, the way or ways in which the activity you listed above has been meaningful or significant for you.

_____

_____

_____

_____

_____

_____

Great! You've just written the thesis sentence for an essay regarding a meaningful activity. Later in this chapter, you'll find some suggestions on how to develop this thesis sentence into a complete essay about an important activity.

Topic 4—Discuss your educational and/or your career objectives.

This question stumps many students. Often it is not easy for students to identify or name their plans for the future. But, for just a minute, think about why you want to go to college. Look back at your Self-Survey results on **Worksheet 2.** What did you learn about yourself as you thought about your answers in such categories as "School Enthusiasm," "Growth Mindset," and "Eagerness for College?" Some of your thoughts may become your answer to a question about your educational goals. Again, go beyond the obvious. Many students say they want to go to college to get a job. But think about those things that you want to learn in college that will make you a better employee or employer.

Now list below three reasons why you want to go to college:

1. _____

2. _____

3. _____

Next, think about your personal and professional goals. Don't be concerned if you have no idea what you want to do when you get older. You may simply want to list the careers you have considered and provide a brief statement explaining why or how you have thought about each field. Maybe friends or family have suggested various career ideas to you and you have thought seriously about a few of those. You can also ask yourself, "If I were paid an excellent salary to do what I like best, regardless of stature or social value, what would I do with my life?" Pondering such issues and questions is often a good starting point to career exploration.

Using the space below, write an answer to the question: What are your thoughts or ideas about your career or professional goals?

_____

_____

_____

_____

_____

_____

_____

But what if the essay question also asks you to list your personal goals? Don't worry; simply think about those aspects of your personal life that college might change or expand. For instance, perhaps you're looking forward to meeting new friends, becoming more independent, learning about a different part of the country, participating in community service, or trying some activity or skill you've never done before. All of those can comprise the personal goals you'd like to accomplish in college.

In the spaces that follow, jot down some ideas about your personal goals.

_____

_____

_____

_____

_____

_____

_____

Topic 5—Name a person who has had a significant influence on you and describe that influence.

Again, go through your memory bank and think of one individual (a friend, family member, teacher, neighbor, coach, clergy, etc.) who has made a real difference in your life. Think about the ways in which this person influenced you or caused you to change. What did this person teach you? What role model or behavioral example did this person set for you? Be specific. Describe particular instances in which this person's influence made you act or think differently than you might have otherwise. And, most importantly, specify exactly why it is that you selected this person. It is not enough to write, "I admire my Uncle Mark because he is a kind person." You must connect the quality of kindness to you. Do you admire Uncle Mark's kindness because it is a quality you are trying to emulate yourself? Or do you see the kindness he displays as similar to but different from the kind acts you do?

You could also choose someone whose influence or example taught you how not to behave. A coach who used shouting and intimidations to motivate. A friend who is so concerned about making a mistake or venturing outside her comfort zone that she has cut herself off from any new experiences. These are also people who may have opened your mind and caused you to reconsider your perspective.

No matter whom you select as your significant influence, the point of the essay is to tell the admission committee something about you. You are simply using the impact and qualities of your significant person to tell your story.

Select an individual who has had a major influence on your life and articulate one aspect about that influence:

_____
_____
_____
_____
_____
_____
_____

Topic 6—Tell us something about yourself that might be helpful to our understanding of you. Or, simply write on a topic of your choice.

Talk about open-ended! The key here is to choose a single aspect about yourself, your background, your family, your activities, or your accomplishments to focus on. Do not try to tell the committee everything there is to know about you in 300 words! It can't be done, and if you try, it is likely to be a boring recital of every award, contest, or honor you ever won. For this response, choose one significant feature, describe it completely and in a compelling fashion, and tell your reader your own reactions or responses. This is the beginning of one student's response:

Something that might not otherwise come through the statistics of this application is that I don't mind getting dirty. Besides being a kid for most of my life, I've worked with a lot of children. From children, I have learned that the point of a puddle is to jump in it, the idea behind clay is to get it under one's fingernails, and walls are constructed to do handstands against.

This student went on to talk about the effect of "getting dirty" on her life. She related various specific instances of the "messy" process of trial and error as it affected her education and her desire for her college education.

By now, it should be clear that a simple listing of awards and accomplishments does not help your reader learn about you. A list of awards is simply a list. If your reader is to gain any sense of the person you are, you must write of your reactions and feelings about your awards or failures, accomplishments or defeats.

OK, now try it yourself. What is one thing you would like a college to know about you?

_____

_____

_____

_____

_____

_____

Topic 7—Describe a significant academic experience. Or, describe a character in fiction, a historical figure, or a creative work that has had an influence on you.

A significant academic experience could be a particular class you liked. Think about why the class was good. Was it the characteristics of the teacher? Was the subject material particularly fascinating? Did you like the assignments? Be specific about the ways that class made you think and grow. A significant academic experience can also be a particular book or project or experiment in which you became totally absorbed. What made the book or project or experiment so challenging, frustrating, or fascinating to you? Finally, an academic experience can be significant because you really worked hard to understand a topic or a concept and finally mastered it. Here's how one student started:

> *Reading Winnie-the-Pooh again in my junior literature class was significant for me. Winnie, you see, is my hero. He never gets down on himself, never panics in a crisis, and fills his living space with hummed tunes and poetry. I learned that superior literature can be simple. I know that important messages in life come from basic as well as complex words. I appreciate the straightforwardness of Winnie-the-Pooh, but also the depth of analysis that is possible within one's imagination and creativity.*

In the space provided, jot down an idea or two about a significant academic experience:

_____
_____
_____
_____
_____
_____

Another way to answer this question is to consider the extent to which you have lived up to your potential as a high school student. Think about yourself as a student. If you have worked up to your potential, write a brief statement about your strengths as a student. For example, were you successful because of your organizational skills? Your willingness to work hard? Your excellent teachers? If you have not yet worked up to your abilities, why not? There may be perfectly valid reasons—illness, learning difficulties, or changes of high schools. Was it a lack of motivation, or did you place a priority on your out-of-school activities? If some real barriers have impeded your success, you should feel comfortable talking about them.

Have you lived up to your potential in high school? Why or why not?

_____
_____
_____
_____
_____
_____

Topic 8—Discuss some issue of personal, local, national, or international concern and its importance to you.

The choices you're given in this prompt—"some issue of personal, local, national, or international concern"—are not as dissimilar as they appear on first reading. The key to your response is to link the issue to yourself, your feelings, and your experiences. You may be concerned about the environment, but unless you have a personal connection to the topic of recycling, for example, your essay may be little more than an objective (and therefore impersonal) discussion of that topic. The best topic for the "issue" essay is one that matters so much to you that you could write an editorial for your school or city paper. The person who reads your response is most likely uninterested in an expository essay; as with every other essay question, you should use your response to say something about you, the topic about whom your reader really wants to know.

As practice, use the following space to tell about an issue that concerns you:

_____

_____

_____

_____

_____

_____

Worksheet 13—Essay Brainstorming

The eight questions provided in *Worksheet 12* commonly appear on college applications; however, as indicated earlier, the possibilities for essay questions are endless. Don't let the questions stump you; remember, the central purpose of the essay, regardless of the specific question, is to let the admission committee get to know you. So, if your applications contain questions not among the eight just discussed, use the following exercises to come up with ideas for answering the uncommon question.

Listed below is a series of adjectives. Quickly circle those words you feel are true about you most of the time.

able	determined	independent	original	respectful
accepting	direct	ingenious	overconfident	responsible
active	diplomatic	innovative	passive	retentive
adaptable	disciplined	inspiring	paternal	scientific
aggressive	doer	intelligent	perceptive	self-reliant
ambitious	driver	introverted	perfectionist	sensible
analytical	efficient	intuitive	persuasive	sensitive
articulate	energetic	jovial	playful	sentimental
assertive	enterprising	kind	pleasant	serious
aware	enthusiastic	knowledgeable	powerful	sincere
brave	extroverted	lazy	practical	skillful
calm	fair	leader	precise	sociable
carefree	flexible	liberal	principled	sophisticated
caring	follower	lively	progressive	spontaneous
cheerful	frank	logical	protective	stable
clever	free	loving	proud	strong
competent	friendly	loyal	punctual	supportive
competitive	genial	maternal	questioning	sympathetic
confident	gentle	mature	quiet	tactful
conforming	giving	merry	radical	thoughtful
conscientious	gregarious	modest	rational	tolerant
cooperative	gullible	methodical	realistic	tough
courageous	happy	naive	reasonable	trustworthy
creative	helpful	negative	reassuring	understanding

critical	honest	nervous	reflective	useful
decisive	honorable	objective	relaxed	vulnerable
demanding	humorous	observant	reliable	wise
dependable	idealistic	optimistic	religious	witty
dependent	imaginative	organized	reserved	workaholic

Which three circled words describe you the best? List them here.

1. _____

2. _____

3. _____

Think about some activities, achievements, failures, and/or experiences in your life that might best illustrate these adjectives. For instance, if the word "caring" describes you well, when was that quality particularly evident? Perhaps you can illustrate your caring qualities by describing your feelings when you helped your friend out of a troublesome situation or the reasons you have a menagerie of stray animals at home. Don't hesitate to think about the negative qualities listed above as well.

It is not enough to simply claim to possess certain qualities; your writing must demonstrate these qualities to your reader. In other words, when the reader is finished with the essay, he or she should be thinking, "What a caring person!" without you ever having to mention the word "caring."

Again, it's your turn. Choose one of the three qualities you listed, and provide a brief illustration of how that quality describes you:

_____

_____

_____

_____

_____

_____

_____

Here's another brainstorming exercise. Complete the following open-ended sentences:

1. People describe me as . . .

_____

_____

_____

_____

_____

2. During my high school days, I have succeeded at . . .

_____

_____

_____

_____

_____

3. During my high school days, I have failed at . . .

_____

_____

_____

_____

_____

4. The thing most often misunderstood about me is . . .

_____

_____

_____

_____

_____

5. An important decision I made in high school was to . . .

_____

_____

_____

_____

_____

Do any of your answers to the above open-ended questions suggest any other potential essay topics? If so, list them below:

_____

_____

_____

_____

_____

_____

Six Strategies for Excellent Essays

1. Watch your structure, grammar, and spelling.

Here are some guidelines:

- Structure your essay so your reader (the college admission staff) gains some sense of an organized flow of ideas. Your organizational plan enables your essay to fulfill a purpose, to go someplace; it gives it a logical beginning, middle, and end.
- Write your body paragraphs first. Don't worry about your introduction until later. Normally, you should decide what you want to talk about and then make a few notes or an outline of how you will develop that topic.
- Write a clear thesis or controlling statement.
- Make sure your grammar is clear and your spelling correct.
- Make your examples specific, specific, specific. An essay that includes colorful, specific details will be interesting to read. Your reader wants to know how you lost the close sailboat race, and you will help bring this to life if you describe how the boat looked and your nervousness or overconfidence on race day. Your writing should be so concrete that your reader can almost see the boat, the race, and the trophy and smell the salt air.

- There is one essential way in which a college essay differs from an essay you might write for an expository writing class. Your college essay should not be written in the third person ("one should realize. . .") or in the second person ("if you are on student council. . ."). Rather, your essay should be written in the first person ("from student council, I learned. . ."). When you write, you should tell your reader, "I felt like a fool as the football slipped through my hands," or "Even though it ruined my 'perfect' GPA, I was more ecstatic about the B that I earned in advanced calculus than any A+ I ever received."

2. Share the good and the bad.

Students often feel that negative, disappointing, or uncomfortable experiences should not be used as the subject of a college essay. Some fear these experiences might reveal a weakness or insecurity and that such information would be a liability for an applicant. Nonsense! A sensitive, but not self-pitying, exploration and explanation of a difficult sophomore year or an uncomfortable camp experience can make a wonderful, insightful essay.

3. Write from the heart.

The more effectively you can show your reader how it felt to have a car accident or make an important decision, the more your reader will know about you—and that is the goal of a good college essay. Colleges want to know about your character and your personality.

4. Make the most of the space you have (and stay within word limits).

Specifications on how long an essay should be vary. The college application usually provides clear instructions. Some essay's (personal statements) are as short as 100 words. Others can ask for essays of 650 words or more. Typically these essays are less than two double-spaced, typed pages! When you think about it, that's not that much space to tell someone about who you are or what an important event/experience meant to you. That's one reason specific detail is so essential; you need to make every word matter.

5. Let your preliminary readers read but not rewrite.

One of the most common questions about essays is whether to have your English teacher or your parents read them. English teachers, while they can be very helpful in reading for grammatical and spelling errors as well as for some content and development issues, tend to read as English teachers do. They are not admission officers, they will not read your essay the same way that an admission offer would, and that difference in perspective is key. That's something to keep in mind if you do have your teacher look over your essays.

As for parents, it may be hard for them to resist the urge to rephrase or restate your ideas in more complex language. They may discourage you from sharing reflections about yourself that may strike them as revealing weakness or insecurity. You are human, as are admission officers, and your human insights make for superior essays.

6. Do not believe the hype that only "highly unusual" essays are read.

Admission committees read all essays (even the ordinary ones). If you're betting that a poem would "really impress them," step back and think about who you are. If creativity or humor or poetry is you, then okay, go for it! If not, do what is honestly you. Creative approaches or stream-of-consciousness ruminations are fine, but only if they meet the primary criterion mentioned earlier—that the essay allows the college to learn about your strengths, your motivations, and your sensitivities.

So, are you ready to tackle an essay topic that one of your colleges lists on its application? If you completed *Worksheet 10*, you should have in front of you a list of the essay questions to which you must respond. Choose one of these topics and do some brainstorming about it, using some of the ideas described in this chapter. Try to formulate a thesis sentence for the essay.

Remember to write your main points and your body paragraphs first; you want to jump write into the "meat" of your essay. See what happens if you write rapidly and without stopping. Try to write at least a page. Do not, at this point, censor your work. Do not stop to correct spelling or look up words. Simply tell your story as if you were writing a letter to a friend. Then, continue writing furiously until you have completed your story. Now go back and draft an interesting introductory paragraph that lays the groundwork for what follows and is so intriguing that the reader can't help but read on. Add a conclusion that doesn't sum up or reiterate what you just told the reader but rather leads him or her to a deeper understanding of what you felt or experienced and its reverberations in your life.

And there it is: a college application essay! Obviously, you'll need to correct grammatical and spelling errors, edit extraneous information, and rewrite in places, but you have a draft of your essay. Does it communicate? Does it say something interesting about you? Is it written honestly and with feeling? Is it completely you? If so, hooray!

Having written your essays, you may be interested in how they fit into everything else the college reviews in making a decision on your application. The next chapter explores the dynamics of the admission process.

Chapter 8
The Admission Process Revealed

The process of selecting students is often cloaked in mystery and intrigue. What goes on behind the closed admission office doors? Why is one student admitted and another rejected? Surely there are some secrets that will help you get admitted. Right? Unfortunately, no. What goes on in admission offices is actually not that mystical.

Think about who these people are and what their task really involves. Admission officers—Dean or Director of Admission, Director of Enrollment, Associate or Assistant Directors, Admission Counselors or Representatives—are professionals whose job it is to recruit and select both the numbers and types of students who will ultimately benefit the college. They are hired to tell the college's story to potential students and then to select, from the pool of people who submit admission applications, those students who are judged most likely to meet the goals of their college. And these goals vary widely. For some colleges, the goal is to admit students who have demonstrated tremendous scholarship and who will benefit from the library holdings and the strengths of the faculty. For others, it is to enroll a freshman class large enough to allow the college to continue to expand and add new departments or programs. Most typically, colleges seek to achieve several objectives when selecting the freshman class.

Admission officers have great sensitivity to individual differences, and therefore, discussions about what a college is "looking for" in a student vary tremendously. Evidence of scholarship or curiosity may mean one thing to one admission officer and something entirely different to another.

Historically, admission offices existed for the purpose of reading applications and making decisions to accept, wait-list, or reject. In recent years, admission offices have directed their efforts more and more on recruiting and attracting students. As a result, competition at selective institutions is more intense than ever. Admission officers who are focusing on student recruitment are doing a good job; the pool of applications to their institutions is increasing, thereby enabling them to select the best qualified (in their eyes) for the spaces available in the class.

Be the Best You

Don't attempt to manipulate the admission process with gimmickry, chicanery, or hocus-pocus. Such strategizing is likely to fail because colleges are well aware of the difference between what's genuine and what's gamesmanship. Don't try to be different just for the sake of being different. There is no essay topic that ensures acceptance, no perfect high school curriculum guaranteed to impress, no person whose opinion of you (expressed in a glowing letter of recommendation) will always sway admission committees. You may hear that you should write an unconventional or wacky essay. You may hear that colleges "love" kids who are star athletes or do community service. You may hear that colleges "always accept" applicants who take Japanese or Esperanto or who enroll in a summer course at a nationally known university. None of these things is necessarily true or always true.

Given that complex, over-the-top strategic maneuvers are of little value, what can you do to ensure you present the best you to the admission officers? Here are some suggestions:

Be yourself.

This may be the most important fact of all when applying to colleges. Tell your story without trying to play the super scholar, the super volunteer, or the super anything! Just tell your own story and tell it well.

Make sure your course load is reflective of your best intellectual efforts.

Be realistic here. Colleges do care what classes you take and what you contribute to those classes. Take the most advanced classes you can manage without getting in over your head. Senior year is no time to slack off. Admission offices are very positive about a strong college preparatory program, with four or five solid subjects each semester. Colleges will admit you primarily on the basis of your ability to be successful doing college-level work. Show the colleges what you are capable of achieving.

Do something productive with your time.

Be as constructive as you can in terms of your extracurricular activities. That arena may be creative arts or leadership or community service or work or sports or a hobby or something else. Admission officers are not likely to be favorably impressed by the hours you devoted to hanging out, updating your status on social media, or playing video games.

Be informed and get involved.

Care about people and issues. Keep up with national or international events or happenings in your city or your school. Learn to articulate your views with reason and even with passion. Follow up on those issues you care most about by volunteering, attending meetings, participating in rallies, or otherwise helping out.

Remember the point made throughout this book: You will have good college choices if you carefully seek out those choices. Don't sit and fret because you may not get into Stanford or Swarthmore or Sewanee. If these colleges are right for you, by all means explore them and apply if they meet your criteria. But if you know that, realistically, you should not reach for the most competitive colleges, be comfortable with your choices. Many people attend lesser-known undergraduate colleges and eventually become political leaders, corporate executives, doctors, lawyers, engineers, teachers. If you must strategize, then do so by finding colleges that, in fact, fit you and will draw out the best within you.

Seven Key Factors That Admission Officers Consider

As indicated previously, colleges consider many factors to select students. Not all of the items listed here are used by all colleges, but they account for most of the input into the eventual college decision. The precise blend of factors varies by college and even by individual members of the admission staff at the same college.

1. High school program

The courses a student takes in high school are often, and correctly, viewed as the most important factor in selecting a freshman class. Colleges look at your list of classes to see where you stand in comparison to other applicants and in comparison to what is offered at your high school. *Your Admission/Readiness Profile* (*Worksheet 4*) provides an indication of how your program compares with others. Admission officers want to see that you have pushed yourself when choosing courses. So take the most challenging program you can handle, including honors or Advanced Placement classes. But know your limits as well. You want to balance the academic, extracurricular, and personal sides of your life.

2. Grades and class rank

Grades provide evidence of your capabilities and motivation, but they are only significant, however, in light of your courses. Sometimes students ask if it is better to take harder classes and get lower grades or easier classes and make higher grades. Unfortunately, this question has no simple answer. Many of the most competitive colleges state that their applicants have taken the most difficult classes and received A's in them. The answer really depends on you. Surely, you should not balk at taking a more advanced class with the fear you might receive a B. Because colleges weigh these factors carefully, it is up to you to select the right program for you. Also important here are the trends in your grades over the years. As for class rank, your school may or may not report rank in class. If it is reported, this information gives colleges another indication of how your performance compares with others at your high school. Of course, high schools vary considerably, and the significance of rank in class will depend on the level of competition at your high school.

3. Test scores

The use of test scores has changed over the last few years. Many colleges have been "test-optional" or "test-flexible" for a long time. "Test-optional" means that the admission process does not require the submission of standardized tests. At these colleges, candidates who submit scores are considered equally with those who do not submit scores. Recently many more colleges have switched to test-optional, primarily as a result of the pandemic, when in-person testing became problematic.

Students should not assume, however, that "test-optional" means that colleges don't care about scores or look at test scores, if available. Instead, it means that the decision to submit your scores or not is up to you. To make that decision, you'll need to assess your strengths as a student and as a test-taker. Strategic use of testing can be a tool in your toolkit as you consider how best to present yourself to colleges.

The two entrance exams used by colleges are the SAT and the ACT. Colleges that require test scores accept either of these tests. If you plan to take a test, determine which of the two is the best test for you. You can make this decision by taking a sample of each test. To do so, search for "which test is better for me? SAT or ACT?"

After taking a practice test or two, you will want to consider a number of factors, keeping in mind that your practice scores could be raised with practice. Do your scores add a dimension to your college application that might not be captured elsewhere? For example, do your scores show strength in areas where your grades (for whatever reason) may not have been stellar? Are your scores almost, but not quite, in line with those of students admitted to colleges you're considering? In any of these circumstances, practicing and taking the SAT or ACT test might serve you well. Note that it is increasingly possible to do test preparation inexpensively through free or low-cost test preparation resources.

Test scores are one indicator that has traditionally been used to assess the likelihood of success as a college freshman. Over the years, however, there has been controversy about the fairness of standardized tests. Citing discrepancies in educational resources and ability to pay for expensive test preparation, many claim that test scores favor more affluent students. Others argue that tests in and of themselves are unreliable and unstable indicators of college success. These critics note that motivation, time management, and organization are the most reliable indicators of achievement in college.

Even before the pandemic, not all colleges viewed test results the same way. Some schools were more "test conscious" than others. Very large universities, for example, often placed more emphasis on test scores because the number of applications they receive made a thorough review of other features less likely. By and large, however, test scores have never been viewed as the critical variable in making admission decisions. Colleges traditionally have given more weight to high school program difficulty and performance than to test scores.

For a listing of college testing policy and information about standardized tests, visit fairtest.org.

Finally, be aware that there may be other situations or circumstances for which colleges will require scores. For example, submission of scores may be required for merit scholarship consideration. Lastly, colleges may also use AP (Advanced Placement) scores, if available, either for admission, for college credit, or to fulfill general education requirements.

4. Extracurricular activities

There is no such thing as the "perfect" list of extracurricular activities. Some students have exhibited extensive involvement with leadership in one or two activities. Other students have a broad set of involvements in several activities. At the most competitive colleges, accepted students have been recognized by their teachers and advisors as having "really made a difference" and often have achieved recognition that extends far beyond their high school or even their community. Admission officers look at extracurricular activities to answer the question "What has this young person done with his or her time?" It is up to you to demonstrate on your application that your activities have been meaningful and noteworthy. Use your *Activities/Experiences Record*, *Worksheet 3*, to help you think about the strength of your activities. (*Worksheet 3* can also be helpful in completing your applications.) Many admission officers would prefer to see a student involved in fewer activities with evidence of sustained commitment than someone who merely joins many clubs and organizations.

5. Personal qualities

Although this factor is hard to define, it certainly plays into the admission decision. Admission officers want to know a prospective freshman as well as possible, and they are looking for evidence of qualities that will contribute to their student body. Qualities such as depth of intellectual curiosity, sustained interest in or commitment to a local or school issue, altruism, fairness, and particularly meaningful reactions to a life experience or a response to a setback can be, and often are, significant. Some students show dedication to community service, others have special talents or abilities. Still others have travel or work experiences. Any of these may catch the eye of an admission officer. Your level of initiative in day-to-day living can be important, and so can an ongoing appreciation for ethical, historical, and world issues. Your college essay and the comments of teachers and others who know you can tell the admission officer about the kind of personal qualities you possess.

6. The application itself and your personal statements or essays

Colleges today typically require students to write statements covering specific topics. Your responses to application questions, particularly essay questions, give admission officers a sense of what is important to you and how you think. They become a "window to your mind." Given their importance in conveying who you are, any time spent on your essays would be time well spent. Essays were discussed in depth in *Chapter 7*.

7. Recommendations

Most colleges require that prospective freshmen ask at least one person who knows them well to complete a recommendation on their behalf. These recommendations are another clue to you as a person and as a student. Give careful thought to those you ask to complete a recommendation form. Your best bets are individuals who know you well and can comment frankly on your intellectual skills as well as your potential. Frequently, your high school counselor is asked to write a recommendation for you, so get to know your counselor as well as you can. Some of the most competitive colleges also ask for teacher recommendations. Don't necessarily select the most popular teacher, the teacher who gave you your highest grade, or the teacher who, according to your classmates, "writes the best recommendations." Pick teachers who really know you and will take time to write insightful, thoughtful, honest letters. Because colleges are evaluating your intellectual potential through your recommendations, letters from "bigwigs" such as the Governor, a leading professional in your community (who may be a graduate of the college), or other well-known persons rarely are helpful—unless the individual has worked with you and can contribute something significant to your admission file. On the other hand, you should not hesitate to ask someone who knows you well—say, an employer or the leader of a summer experience—to write a letter on your behalf. These letters have the potential of helping the admission staff know you better. But consider your recommenders carefully. Too many recommenders can be distracting and work against you.

Although these seven factors are the ones most commonly considered by admission officers in deciding on new freshmen, there are other considerations. Colleges also look for evidence of your motivation as well as your ability to overcome adversity. The most selective colleges seek those who are best able, by virtue of their intelligence and maturity, to make full use of the resources—teachers, equipment, libraries, and so on—the college provides. Your level of interest in the college also might have an influence on your admission decision.

It is important to remember, however, that surefire admission formulas seldom exist. Students often ask, "What GPA do I need to be admitted?" Parents want to know, "Which activities look best to admission officers?" While a few universities (typically, those that are large and state-supported) actually use an admission index that consists of some combination of grades and test scores, most admission decisions are multifaceted and therefore hard to predict. No college ranks every applicant and then accepts a certain percentage of students. If you have completed *Your Admission/Readiness Profile* (*Worksheet 4*) realistically and honestly and have read the section on *"Determining Your Likelihood of Admission"* in *Chapter 5*, you should have some sense of how you might compare with other applicants.

Behind the Scenes

Remember that admission officers take all of the factors described above into consideration. Therefore, raising your semester grades from B+ to A-, while significant, does not automatically mean your chances of getting into a very competitive college suddenly go from fair to good since your course load, demographic characteristics, activities, and so on likely have not changed. Similarly, an outstanding essay will not compensate for a weak program of classes or little evidence of commitment to academics. So while score improvements and spending time on your college essay are important, keep in mind that admission officers consider the full complement of factors as they read applications for admission.

Central to this discussion is the realization that colleges admit students for many different reasons and with different admission portfolios. The most competitive colleges are seeking a diverse and "balanced" class. They seek some students because of their scholastic credentials alone and others because of what they bring to the campus in terms of unique perspectives, skills, and interests. One student may be favorably considered primarily because of top grades and several involvements. Another student may be admitted because of musical or athletic talents; some hail from geographic areas underrepresented at that college. **Most very selective colleges weigh factors carefully. They may want first-generation college students.** Although there is evidence that this is changing, they may respond favorably to sons or daughters of their alumni. The US Supreme Court, in the early 2000's, affirmed the ability of colleges to consider race as one factor in making admission decisions. The position of the court is controversial and is likely to be reconsidered. Typically, none of these qualities (alumni, geographic diversity, athletic talents, children of university employees, etc.) guarantees a student's admission; however, all of them figure into the total picture, and one quality may tip the scales in favor of a particular student.

Given all of these factors—the qualities that students bring, the college's interest in building a balanced class—it is important to remember that admission decisions are not, by definition, fair and equitable. Admission officers are fallible individuals who make purposefully subjective decisions. What may grab the attention of one admission officer may not even raise an eyebrow of someone else. The way one college elects to balance a class may be different from another school's approach. Furthermore, the relative weight of test scores, essays, or extracurricular activities varies widely from one college to the next—even among colleges perceived as similar in their level of admission difficulty.

As an applicant, then, your best game plan is to approach the college choice process realistically. As stated before, you do have choices and you should concentrate on colleges where you will "fit in." "Fitting in" is always more important than "getting in." In terms of "getting in," you should focus on colleges where you perceive you have a reasonable chance of admission. Sure, have one or two "reach" colleges (where your chance of admission is less, but still possible), but spend the majority of your time on those schools where your background and skills suggest a good chance of admission. Don't become unglued because there are a few colleges where you will likely not be admitted. As stated in **Chapter 1**, be happy because more than 2,500 colleges do want you! Success in a college that is a good match for you is what really counts.

Dealing With Admission Decisions: Accept, Deferral, Reject, Wait-list

The end of the college planning process involves making the decision of which college you will attend. Part of that decision may have been made for you . . . by the colleges to which you applied. Your thoroughness likely has led to appropriate college choices and acceptance letters from colleges that really fit you and where you can make a contribution. If so, congratulations are in order. The sequence of events discussed in this section frequently occurs in February, March, and April of your senior year.

Before you receive decision letters from your colleges, you need to think about your priority list. What school is your first choice? Second choice? As you know by now, the process of college planning involved considering high-, medium- and low-chance-of-admission schools. Even if you haven't visited your schools, you can use the information gleaned from your research to make some decisions. Which is your favorite high-chance school? Medium-chance? Low-chance? Talk to your parents about your choices. What schools do they like for you? Why?

Acceptance Letters

You will receive one of four letters from colleges: an acceptance, a deferral, a rejection, or a wait-list notification. If you are offered admission, congratulations!

You may want to visit or revisit the schools to which you've been accepted to in order to finalize your decision. No schools require you to provide a housing deposit before May 1, but with big state schools (where housing may be tight), it's best to ensure housing early. As soon as you know what school you want to attend, send in your deposit. Even though you're admitted to college, don't slack off on your grades; schools have been known to retract their offer if a student's grades fall significantly. Lastly, you should send a letter or e-mail to the other schools that accepted you (letting them know your decision); it's the right thing to do.

Deferral Letters

Students who are deferred are reevaluated later in the admission cycle; in other words, they are told, "We need more time to make a decision." If you are still interested in the college, let the admissions office know of the specific reasons why the college is a good match for you. In other words, demonstrate your interest. Some students send additional letters of recommendation, mid-year grade report, or other materials that might strengthen their admission profile. Colleges vary in their openness to receiving additional information and so you want to be sure to understand the deferral policy of the college. This is also a good time to consult with your college counselor.

Rejection Letters

If the letter you receive is a rejection, you will feel disappointed. A denial letter hurts, and nothing said here is likely to ease the pain. It is tempting to suggest that the college is really not the best fit and your other choices are more appropriate. It is also tempting to say that the admission process is sometimes unfair and that good students are often left without an acceptance while others, perceived as less well qualified, have gained admission. Both of these statements, while perhaps truthful, overlook the true feelings that are present whenever such a setback hits.

If you have been rejected by a college, it's practically impossible not to take a letter of rejection personally. It may help if you bear in mind the following facts. Never has admission to college been as difficult as in the last few years. Furthermore, admission is a subjective and sometimes unpredictable process. Admission directors often state that the process is imprecise, subjective, and seldom reflective of who will be most successful in life.

What drives selective admission decisions today is what the college needs, not what any individual applicant possesses. Don't let a college admission office dictate your worth as a student or as an individual. The most important thing is to rally and move forward quickly. Arrange to visit schools and be prepared to make a decision by May 1. Reactions to such setbacks distinguish a person with character and grit from those who whine and lose their confidence. Your ability to handle a denial with guts says a great deal about you as a person and will help you be a successful college student wherever you decide to attend.

The Wait-List

Receiving a letter offering you a place on the wait-list can feel like being stuck in limbo. This is the most complex alternative because it is so tenuous and uncertain, and it is difficult—indeed impossible—to predict the outcome. The number of people accepted off the wait-list varies dramatically from school to school and from year to year. If you are placed on a waiting list, "keep calm and carry on." This is an important decision-making time, and you need to be rational as you figure out your next move.

First, it is imperative that you *evaluate the schools to which you were offered admission and decide which of them you want to attend*. It is neither feasible nor appropriate to wait to hear from the wait-list college(s) before deciding. Indeed, most schools don't know if they will have a space until well after May 1. Sometimes students feel a college is "better"—more selective, for example—if it wait-listed them instead of admitting them. Please accept the reality of the situation. If a student applies to two equal colleges, one school might accept the student and the next might wait-list or reject the student. The admission decision has no relevance to academic excellence of the colleges. Visit your accepted schools (a second time, if necessary), and decide where you will attend. Once you have made your choice, send in a deposit to secure your place for the fall. Some wait-listed students are happy with their choice of colleges that accepted them and remove their names from the wait-list so they can move on. You may choose to do the same. On the other hand, if you feel strongly that your wait-list school is a good match for you, you may want to "pursue the wait-list." Think about ways to demonstrate your continuing interest in the school. Two ideas to consider are sending a letter of continued interest and submitting your most current grades (if outstanding). Talk to your high school counselor about these and other options. Keep in mind that at most colleges, there is no way to calculate chances of getting off a wait-list. As such, you need to be OK with a period of ambiguity.

No college is perfect, and while it's tempting to believe that College X or University Y is your dream school, the truth (as has been stated many times in this book) is that wonderful opportunities await you at many colleges. It will be wonderful if you are accepted at your first-choice school, but if you are not, it is important that you put that outcome into perspective, rebound, and make your college years—wherever you attend—meaningful and successful. The next chapter focuses on the important skills, perception, and attitudes that will help you do just that.

Chapter 9
Being Successful In Your Freshman Year (and Beyond)

Beginning your collegiate experience may bring on a number of emotions: enthusiasm and fear are two of the most common. You may feel enthusiasm because you are beginning a new chapter in your life. This new chapter may allow you to continue a successful high school career and reach new heights. Or it may give you the opportunity for a fresh start with people who don't have preconceived notions about your potential. You may feel fear because college is a new experience, and new experiences are often approached with a certain amount of trepidation and uncertainty. You will be leaving your familiar surroundings and entering a community that will present new people, new circumstances, and new stresses.

It is important to that you balance your studies and academic-success needs with your fun and relationship needs. Successful college students know—or, more commonly, learn—how to achieve this balance. It takes time to make a complete adjustment to deciding your own schedule and setting your own priorities. Some argue that you need a full year of college to make a total adjustment.

This chapter is designed to give you a few pointers that may help contribute to success in college. But there are no easy answers and no recipe to "cook up" a successful college career. Because everyone is different, some of the following ideas may be valuable to you and others may not be. Use what you find helpful as you approach the challenges and excitement of your freshman year.

Attitude

1. Make a commitment to succeed.

It sounds simple, but often, at the heart of unsuccessful college students is a lack of commitment to academic success.

2. Make academic success your top priority.

No one can do that for you. There will be plenty of time for fun, but your obligation, first and foremost, is to your intellectual development and growth. You also have an obligation to your parents to graduate in four years.

3. Don't sit back waiting for the college to be "exciting."

You make it happen. Get out. Meet new people. Get involved. College, like life, is what you make it.

4. Remember that there will always be ups and downs during your college years.

During big changes in our lives (such as starting college), our emotions can become exaggerated. Give things time to fall into place. Allow time to get to know people. Most students are not able to fully evaluate their college experience until the spring of their freshman year. There will always be good days and bad days, great experiences and lousy ones. On your bad days, learn to relax, maintain your equilibrium, and move forward. Don't let one low grade or a negative comment from your roommate throw you into a tailspin.

5. Anticipate homesickness.

You have left your home, your family, and your friends. You will miss them. Don't try to pretend homesickness is not there. Experiencing homesickness does not suggest weakness. Share your feelings with others, and maintain regular contact with home. It might help to bring a piece of home with you—pictures of friends and family, your yearbook, posters, etc.

6. Learn to tolerate some degree of bureaucracy.

Be prepared for the runaround. Ask two or three people the same question before you are certain of an answer.

7. Be ready to put up with a lack of privacy.

Residence hall rooms are often small, and cramped spaces can mean short fuses. Use your space wisely. Live in your room, but also find a way to live outside of your room by going to the library, the dorm lounge, or the student center.

8. Stand up for your own values and preferences.

Don't succumb to peer pressure. Be true to your self. People respect those with conviction.

9. Think about the type of person you want to be in college.

The "high school you" may be different from the "college you." Do you want to be known as a scholar? Leader? Follower? Person with values? Bystander? Party animal? It is up to you to make these choices.

10. Before leaving for college, talk with your parents and friends about how they see your adjustment in the first few weeks of college.

How do they feel you will react to a new and unknown situation? Such insights from those you know and respect can help improve your chances for a smooth transition.

Academics

1. Seek help immediately if you feel you don't understand a particular class.

With only a few graded assignments per term, waiting to see how you do on the next test (or paper) may be too late. It's up to you. There will not be any calls home, progress reports, etc. It's up to you to stay on top of your work. Many professors tend to be slightly subjective in handing out grades; the more you meet with them, the more likely they are to remember you come grading time.

2. Work hard to get good grades from the beginning of your college days.

A low grade point average after one semester puts tremendous pressure on you later.

3. Meet with professors!

Schedule an appointment or drop by and introduce yourself during their posted office hours. And find at least one professor during your freshman year with whom you feel comfortable talking to about the ins and outs of the school, your career, etc.

4. Go to class!

Research studies have shown that academic success is as dependent on class attendance as on the amount of time spent studying.

5. Teachers are people, too!

If you've enjoyed a class, tell the instructor. Keep in touch with teachers or administrators you like. They can become friends who can "show you the ropes" and possibly help you later with a recommendation for a job or graduate school.

6. Select your courses well, but don't be afraid to drop a course if it's too much for you.

The ability to drop a class is a major benefit to college. However, learn the official college procedures for dropping classes and follow them or you may wind up with an F on your record.

Using Resources

1. Being independent doesn't mean you have to do everything yourself.

Seek help when you need it.

2. Speak up.

Don't let course difficulties, roommate problems, homesickness, etc., back you into a corner. Let someone know. Take action. Colleges are filled with people who are paid to help you.

- The Counseling Center can help you cope with homesickness, test anxiety, relationship problems, and general adjustment difficulties.
- The Dean of Students office can answer questions about getting involved in activities and general questions about how the college operates.
- Your Resident Advisor or Resident Assistant is just down the hall and can help you deal with roommates, excessive dorm noise, homesickness, etc., as well as offer suggestions for meeting people and settling in on campus.
- A Peer Counselor can provide support with college adjustment as well as advice about good professors.

- Your Academic Advisor is the person to go to for advice about your schedule, classes, workload, choice of major, and career ideas.
- The Health Center can take a throat culture, write a prescription, set up counseling, and provide care for your physical ailments.
- Religious Services, Chaplaincy, Student Ministries, and other resources provide support and spiritual fellowship.
- The Financial Aid office has information on scholarships, loans, and work opportunities.

3. Talk to juniors and seniors who know their way around, both the campus and the bureaucracy.

Quiz them about good courses and great professors, the least busy laundry rooms on campus, the best places nearby to shop for basics, cheap but good restaurants, and anything else that will make you feel more at home.

Courses, Majors, and Careers

1. Be patient.

Don't come unglued if you listed mathematics as your major on your application and now, as a freshman, you are absolutely certain you don't want to major in math. Freshman programs typically are quite similar; most freshmen students take general courses required for graduation. Discuss the fact that you are not sure about your major with your advisor, and sign up for classes that are required of all students. During your first year, you need not worry too much about picking a major.

2. Make a distinction between "major" and "career."

A major is an academic field you like and want to learn more about. A career is the life work you choose to pursue after college. Many students who ultimately go on to medical school choose undergraduate majors in English or French; lots of students who go on to graduate business school choose undergraduate majors in chemistry or philosophy. Take courses that interest you, broaden your knowledge, and maximize your chances of success.

3. Don't feel compelled to make a career choice immediately.

Again, be patient. Sample lots of courses and disciplines. Actively explore potential career possibilities. Take advantage of opportunities for part-time jobs or internships in career fields of interest. In addition, ask teachers about job opportunities in their subject areas, and use the career planning office for an interest assessment and for information.

Other People

1. Anticipate different lifestyles.

Most students find much more diversity in college when compared to high school. These differences are in areas such as race, ethnicity, sexual orientation, income level, first-generation status, cultural background and gender.

Be ready to communicate with your roommate to resolve problems. Remember, learning to resolve conflicts with roommates and others is a good start to honing your ability to resolve other "people problems" in life. Be open when it comes to differences—and willing to learn. You may have to negotiate some issues by talking them out. Don't hold your feelings inside; express them with tact and consideration. Find other friends in addition to your roommate.

2. Try not to be intimidated by all the new people.

Don't be afraid of all the differences—socio-economic, family, religion, political opinion—you will encounter. View these differences as opportunities to broaden your horizons and be open to them. You may find you have more in common with other students than you first thought. Remember, everyone is new, not just you. Capitalize on this and make lots of friends.

3. When you find yourself in a group of people and you feel uncomfortable, realize that others in the group feel exactly the same way.

Introduce yourself to someone you do not know. Ask that person some questions. Begin and continue a conversation. Work at listening and accepting others; the first step to being accepted is to accept others.

4. Give new friendships time to grow.

Remember that new friends can't immediately fill the gap left by separation from long-standing friendships. Be patient.

5. Share your goals with your roommate or others you trust.

Say to your roommate, "I'm working toward a 3.0 this semester. I need your help in achieving this goal." Openness, cooperation, and sharing help you achieve your goals.

6. Don't eat alone. Introduce yourself to someone.

Other students may also feel lonely in the first few weeks of school. This is the time to branch out and make new friends.

Time Management

1. Time will fly by faster in college than it ever has.

Keep this in mind and make a plan for how you will spend each day. Know how long things take to accomplish.

2. Time is the one commodity everyone in college possesses equally.

Students who use those 24 hours wisely are typically the ones who end up successful.

3. Your schedule for accomplishing tasks may not resemble someone else's schedule.

You need to know yourself and your work pace well enough to be able to determine how long it takes you to write a five-page paper or read 50 pages. Allow enough time to get your work done.

4. Keep up with your assignments each day.

Most often, college students are not given assignments on a daily basis. Rather, you will receive assignments for an entire term. It's up to you to determine what needs to be done daily so you will not be cramming for midterms or finals and pulling all-nighters to get that paper in.

5. Utilize the library and other relatively quiet places on campus to study.

You'll get more done in a shorter time than in your dorm room. Sometimes even getting away from your computer or your phone for a few hours can re-energize you for studying.

6. Use your daylight hours wisely.

Try to get as much studying done during the day as possible, because at night it can be hard to tell friends you can't go out with them.

7. Understand the extent of your scheduled hours.

Scheduled hours are those over which you have no control, for example, class time, team practice time, and dining hall hours. Knowing your scheduled hours will help you plan your unscheduled hours (such as studying, sports, texting, spending time on the computer, phoning, and being with friends).

8. Allow yourself enough time for sleep.

This may sound silly and unnecessary, but college students are prone to wear themselves out by not sleeping enough.

9. Discipline your time by balancing study sessions with social outings.

Learn to say "no." You may need to tell your friends, "I'm not going to the party tonight because I'm going to study." There will always be another party. There won't be another chance for a successful freshman year.

10. Plan your study schedule carefully.

For completing major tasks, one or two hours of concentrated time will be more productive than one or two hours of interrupted time. Figure out the best times and places where you can focus on your studies in a quiet environment with no interruptions (or temptations).

11. Know where your time is going.

You may be surprised to find that your time usage is not what you think it is—or what it ought to be. TV, Netflix, YouTube, video games, Instagram, telephone apps, texting, cards, a romance, etc., can eat up HOURS, leaving you wondering, "Where did all my time go?!?"

12. Keep a calendar.

Note important academic dates—when tests are scheduled, when papers are due, and so on. On long-term projects—such as a term paper—break the assignment up into small segments and establish your own due dates along the way. For example, what is your goal (due date) for finishing the background reading? For writing the first draft? List all of these dates on your calendar. By working steadily on long projects, you will avoid having to do all the work in one night.

13. Limit your time online.

Hours can go by while you are browsing the web, playing games, answering e-mails, following social media, etc. Know your priorities.

Other Areas

1. Your personal safety on campus is your responsibility.

Crimes occur on every campus, urban or rural, large or small. Be careful about where and when you walk at night, keep your room locked, and be accountable for your personal belongings. Do not expect the college to be responsible for you or your possessions.

2. Participate in extracurricular activities.

Studies show that the more "connected" you are to a college, the more fun and successful your experience will be. Connectedness most often comes from a commitment to a group or an organization. Think about two or three activities you want to explore when you arrive on campus. Remember, however, that your activities should be somewhat limited your first year—particularly if you are concerned about your ability to stay on top of your studies. Academics do come first.

3. Roll with the punches.

What if you don't get into your first-choice fraternity or sorority? What if you don't make the tennis team? Such experiences can initially be devastating, but again, deal with your hurt and move on. Learning to overcome or deal with setbacks can be a valuable life skill. Find other groups to join and other ways to use your out-of-class time.

4. Don't live a virtual life.

Carefully consider whether the electronics you bring with you (video game consoles, TV, audio and video streaming, computers, etc.) are enriching your campus life or giving you an excuse to be a hermit. You'll only find friends and activities you enjoy if you seek them out.

5. Don't get wrapped up in trying to have the "typical college experience," whatever that stereotype means to you.

There are countless different types of college experiences, shaped by who you are and where you are going to college. Your experience may differ from that of your parents or your friends at other schools.

6. Keep a journal of your college years.

It is amazing how much you will do and how much of it you can forget.

7. Stay in touch with your parents.

They care about you, are interested in what you're doing, and will be grateful if you share your collegiate experiences with them.

College is a wonderful time of your life. It is filled with new experiences, new ideas, and new discoveries. Your success in college is not a function of your high school grades or your activity list. It is a function of your determination, motivation, organization, and ability to handle new situations. Go for it!

The next chapter focuses on the important role your parents play in your college decision-making. While it is written for your parents, you should read it as well. It may enable you to see the college planning process from their point of view and provide perspectives on some of the issues you may be talking about at home.

Chapter 10

Parents as Educators In the College Selection Process

The process of identifying, researching, and ultimately selecting a college should involve the entire family, and throughout this book, students have been encouraged to discuss their thinking with their parents. While the rest of this book has been directed toward the student, this chapter is written for parents. So the "you" in this chapter refers to parents!

College admission in the twenty-first century is very different than it was when you considered colleges. The population of students seeking admission has exploded, and the nature of college selection itself has changed dramatically. Consider the following example. In 1932, 1,300 students applied to Yale University and more than 70% were admitted. Of these, many graduated from elite, East Coast preparatory schools, and about one quarter were sons of Yale graduates. Today, Yale receives applications from almost 50,000 students per year and admits less than 5% of these applicants. Furthermore, the admitted students come from a wide range of high schools and are diverse in multiple ways.

Because of these and other changes, your role as the parent of a college-bound student is a difficult one. You must consider so many issues, emotions, and contradictory advice. Often parents can feel as overwhelmed as their sons and daughters. But like your student, you should approach this college-seeking process with systematic persistence. Move, with your child, through the various stages of choosing a college as they are presented in this book.

Your role as counselor, advisor, and helper will aid your prospective college student in growing and learning through this process, but it is imperative that your teen take the lead. Seeking your advice and help is advised, but ultimately, your teen must be responsible for the decision. If a parent takes over the process of choosing, the student doesn't learn. If the parent is excessively anxious, the student will act likewise.

You want your son or daughter to make a good decision, and you have worked hard over the years to enable your young person to attend college. Be clear about your expectations, but give your teen space to contemplate the issues involved in choosing a college and in making the right decision. A professional in the field once said of adolescents, "I've been working with this age group for some years now, and I've learned they're a lot like flowers: they need nurturing but they also need to be left alone."

Commonly Asked Questions

Let's begin by discussing eight common questions from parents as they and their students begin to think about college.

Question 1. "My daughter can't plan for college. She doesn't even know what she wants to study! Is it important for my daughter to know what she wants to do in life?"

While this concern is common and well-intentioned, parents and students alike should view college planning as a process significantly different from career planning. In the truest sense, the undergraduate years are intended as a time for self-discovery and intellectual discovery. One of the best approaches to selecting an eventual course of study (a major) and/or a career is to identify the subjects and classes in which a student has interest and the intellectual and personal talents or gifts that the student possesses. Although it is difficult for a high school senior to make the leap from identifying favorite subjects to choosing a career path, let your daughter's likes and dislikes play a role in her initial major selection. But keep in mind, an art major can wind up in medical school, and an English literature major can become a clinical psychologist.

Try to set aside (at least for now) any concerns you have about your daughter's lack of career direction. If she has no idea about potential careers, she may want to look at colleges that offer a broad range of academic programs (a liberal arts and sciences emphasis) so she can keep her options open while making a decision. On the other hand, if she has a sense for what she would like to study, that's great, too. Remember, though, the typical college student changes his or her major at least twice during a four-year college program. What is important is that your daughter actively explores different career possibilities during her undergraduate years. This is accomplished by taking a wide variety of courses, asking teachers about vocations in their fields, participating in internships, using vacations for work experiences in career areas of interest, and utilizing the resources (such as the career planning office) available on college campuses.

By the way, many colleges ask students to declare a major field on their admission application. If your daughter remains undecided, she can simply choose a subject of interest without feeling as though she's locking herself into a definitive career path.

Question 2. "We want our son to attend a college we've heard of—after all, when he gets out in the 'real world,' the name of his alma mater will be the ticket to employment. Right?"

Not necessarily. This question can be answered on two levels. First, as mentioned in *Chapter 1*, the United States has approximately 4,000 colleges. Name recognition varies by area and industry. In other words, parents living in Connecticut employed by the hospitality industry will likely recognize a different set of colleges than will parents living in New Mexico employed by the aerospace industry. Oh, but you ask, "Aren't the Ivy League colleges the 'best'? Wouldn't any prospective employer give an absolute edge to an Ivy League grad?" No, on both counts.

First, a college's membership in the Ivy League Athletic Conference is no guarantee of academic or social fit for any given student. Most importantly, though, perceptions among potential employers about any given college are almost as variable as the employers themselves. No study that has determined that Ivy League graduates have a lock on positions of wealth or power or prestige or influence in our society.

As mentioned earlier, employers are increasingly interested in knowing what any given student has "done" at his or her college. Academic success is reflected by grades, research, independent study, study abroad, honors, and special projects. Social success is evidenced by leadership, participation, and commitments to activities, people, and projects. In the end, these accomplishments matter far more than the name of the school the student lists on a resume. Significantly, a study supported by the U.S. Department of Education found that the name or prestige of the college a student attends has very little influence on future earning potential. "What you do in college does make a big difference," the study reported. In fact, evidence published by Ernest T. Pascarella and Patrick T. Terenzini in their book *How College Affects Students* suggests that only 1% to 2% of the differences in income after graduation are attributable to the specific college a student attends. But, you ask, "Won't the name of a college open doors and create contacts for my son?" Yes, that is probably true. Friendships formed in college are likely to be lifelong. But every college— not just the Ivy League—has an alumni network accessible to its new graduates. Doors are open to those who achieve at a high level in the college they attend. Help your son choose a school that will facilitate that achievement and result in feelings of accomplishment.

You must also realize that the admission process has become increasingly competitive and not just within the Ivy League. Even the most stellar high school resume is no guarantee of admission at the "name" schools. Every year, colleges and universities are seeing record numbers of applicants for limited spaces. In a recent year, New York University had almost 100,000 applications for its New York City campus, where there are spaces for less than 6,500 freshmen. The University of California, Los Angeles (UCLA) received more than 165,000 applications for a recent freshman class. It admitted fewer than 15% of those who applied and is even more competitive for out-of-state students. In this era of such intense competition among the most selective colleges, pushing for a big name college (public or private) can lead to tears or feelings of failure. Even worse, it takes the emphasis away from what should be the appropriate focus of college planning: where will a young person be successful and happy in his or her undergraduate years?

Question 3. "We want our daughter to attend a 'better' school than we did. Are we wrong?"

No, and this concern is well-intentioned. A generation ago, students' college decisions were often made for them, either by their own parents ("you will go to the local college!") or because of finances ("we simply can't afford another school") or because college choices were simply not known. Furthermore, there was not the same perception that college selection involved choice. (The age of information and marketing has made college options and the information about them increase at an explosive rate.) So, looked at one way, this question may revolve around the way parents made their own college decisions. Share with your daughter how you decided to attend the college that you did. If you did not attend college, talk with your daughter about your thoughts and dreams when you left high school.

Another aspect of this question relates to issues of prestige and goals that you may have for your daughter. Some parents so burden their children with their own unfulfilled dreams that they pressure their children to apply to prestigious colleges so that they themselves will be perceived positively. Please have appropriate dreams and goals for your daughter. Share those dreams with her, but distinguish them from your own aspirations. Be careful that your student uses your perceptions only as information in the formulation of her own unique goals and aspirations. Help your daughter discover and name her talents and gifts, and then point her in directions that will give her opportunities to develop them.

Also, work to respect the differences between you and your daughter. Do not assume your wonderful experience at a particular type of college would fit your daughter as well.

The appropriate college choice for your young person is the college where she will be able to enjoy success—an important ingredient in the development of self-esteem. Remember, it is your daughter, not you, who will spend hours and days in the classroom and in the library. Help her make those hours enjoyable and rewarding, not filled with struggle, frustration, and tears, simply because she made a college decision for you and not herself.

Finally, once your daughter does make a college decision, affirm her choice. Spare her from feeling guilty if she happens to make a choice that would not be yours. Help her know her choices are acceptable to you. A college choice is rarely "right" or "wrong" in the abstract. In fact, it is clear to those advising young people in college choice that adolescents really do know what is best for themselves. They will tell us, if only we listen.

Question 4. "Our son hasn't been too successful in high school, so we don't want to spend much for his college education. Wouldn't we just be throwing money down the drain?"

At its core, this concern views the amount of money spent on college tuition as a reward or punishment for performance. While practicality may suggest this position is logical, parents are advised to view the college experience not as a product with a price tag affixed, but rather as a process whose benefits are without price. An inexpensive college is no more likely to provide a successful college experience for a late bloomer than an expensive one. The most important concerns should be your son's match to the college and the ability of the college environment to provide the qualities and people necessary for your son to succeed.

Question 5. "How do I deal with images and perceptions about colleges?"

There are so many images about colleges, and the grapevine seems to continue to work overtime! Here are a few perceptions, some serious, some tongue-in-cheek.
"Only a big school can be fun."
"The best colleges are in the East."
"Without fraternities and sororities, my son won't have a social life."
"The College of the Sun is a party school."
Students can have a great deal of fun at a small school; many would even contend that the absence of fraternities and sororities is a guarantee of a social life. No school is entirely a party school, nor is any school entirely a grind school. Students will surely find parties and grinds at every school if they seek those kinds of experiences.
"The College of the Urbanites is dangerous because it is located in a city."
"My daughter will have nothing to do at The University of the Ruralites because it is located in a small town."

Not every urban campus is dangerous, nor every small town a bore. Students in city locations do need to take common-sense precautions, as do those attending schools in suburbs and small towns. Small towns across the country vary a great deal, as do the colleges located in them. Some college towns have a rich array of activities, events, shops, and restaurants dedicated to serving the student population.

Some perceptions are based on experience and some on hearsay or outdated notions. Verify what you hear with reliable information. Be wary of blanket statements about any given school or area of the country. And be cautious about accepting such stereotypes from your son or daughter.

Question 6. "Admission decisions seem so irrational and unpredictable. What's going on?"

Admission is a complex process but not a mystical one. Rarely does one factor—such as one or two B's on an otherwise all A transcript—in and of itself cause a student to be denied or accepted. As described in *Chapter 8*, admission committees carefully and thoughtfully consider many dimensions of each applicant when they admit a class, and it is difficult to predict who will get into one school from one year to the next. Therefore, the fact that one student was admitted one year with a particular GPA means very little for admission of another student with a similar GPA the following year. More importantly, many factors are considered. Be cautious of parents who talk about the SAT scores or grade point averages or stellar recommendations of students who gained or were denied admission to certain colleges. That's simply the grapevine at work! Students and parents rarely know all the details contained in another student's admission folder.

In addition, the admission picture for any given school changes from year to year depending on the number of applications received for the freshman class and the qualities sought for that incoming class. Most importantly, you do not know whether the college that matched a friend's child also matches the needs of your child. As hard as it may be, parents need to assess their student objectively in light of the criteria available from most counselors. *Worksheet 4, Your Admission/Readiness Profile*, can help you assess how your son or daughter compares with other students.

Although every parent would like to believe that his or her son or daughter is simply tops (and should be in your eyes), admission committees inevitably see a young person in light of the thousands of other applications they read each year. The U.S. has more than 30,000 high schools, and many have a valedictorian. Many of those 30,000 valedictorians apply to the 100 most selective colleges in the nation. And it is increasingly common for students to score over 700 on the critical reading and the math sections of the SAT or, in this day of grade inflation and weighted grades, attain a grade point average of 4.0 or higher.

Question 7. "My daughter's counselor can't tell us what the precise requirements are for admission at a particular college. Shouldn't he or she know if the college requires, say, a 3.2 grade average and an SAT score of 1200?"

Few colleges admit according to a strict formula. In making their admission decisions, most colleges weigh all the factors discussed in *Chapter 8*, e.g., strength of the student's program, recommendations, test scores, activities, and evidence of intellectual curiosity. What your counselor should be able to give you is some indication of your daughter's admission chances, based on his experience with other students applying to that college. You can also assess your student's chances by reading the section in *Chapter 5* titled *"Guidelines for Determining Your Likelihood of Admission."*

The place of test scores in college admission is changing. Many colleges have made test scores optional. If your student is a good test taker, or is likely to be, submitting scores will be a positive. If in doubt, students are encouraged to do some test preparation and sit for either the ACT or the SAT. The student's decision to submit can be made later.

Question 8. "Our daughter will likely go to graduate school, so why should it matter where she gets her undergraduate degree?"

Where your daughter goes to graduate or professional school (law, medicine, graduate school, etc.) may be essential to her training, education, and career prospects. Don't disregard the importance of her undergraduate choice, however. With regard to undergraduate education, studies consistently demonstrate that these are formative years for young people and a time of intense personal growth and development. This is when students are apt to find their place, learn more about themselves and others, establish their limits, and develop friendships and interactions with all kinds of people. As undergrads, students move from dependence on the family to independence. Undergraduates learn from their mistakes and figure out how to deal with both their strengths and their weaknesses. During these critical undergraduate years, young people learn to balance life commitments, self-motivate, resolve interpersonal conflicts, problem-solve, work cooperatively with a team, and hone their time management skills.

Colleges are highly diverse places, and for many students, this may be the first time they encounter individuals not only from other regions of the United States but also from other nations. Understanding different perspectives and hearing the opinions of others promote solid decision-making and potentially better parenthood and citizenship. During their undergraduate years, many students establish a positive approach to learning or a "growth mindset," a term popularized by Stanford professor Carol Dweck. In the *Psychology Today* article "15 Ways to Build a Growth Mindset," author Tchiki Davis explains, "A growth mindset is simply the belief that our basic abilities can be developed and improved through dedication and hard work. It's not so much that this belief is some kind of magic. It's just that without a growth mindset, we don't exert the required effort and so we remain perpetually stuck."

Graduate or professional school is primarily about academics. Students prepare for a career. While it is true that the undergraduate years are also about academics and initial preparation for a vocation, these years also focus on personal and social growth. So as you think about what's best for your daughter, don't downplay her choice of an undergraduate school; it's likely to be the place where she develops her self-awareness and forges the skills that will contribute to her being all she is capable of being as a young adult.

Your Proper Level of Involvement

Choosing a college should be a family decision, with the student in the driver's seat. In fact, parents ought to look on the college admission and decision-making process as an educational opportunity. A student who makes a college decision makes one of the most critical decisions in his or her life. Like most decisions, it should be made strategically and systematically, not haphazardly or whimsically.

Sadly, many students come to the college decision with little or no experience at major decision-making. As a parent, one of the most valuable gifts you can give your son or daughter is to demonstrate how to arrive at a thoughtful decision and give them practice—even from a very young age—at making decisions, first small choices and then larger ones. Parents can also empower their students by giving them strategies for solving problems and then stepping back to allow them to take the lead in the college admission process. Students—not parents—should arrange college visits, request applications and catalogues, and take responsibility for completing their applications (including essays and personal statements) and submitting them on time. Do help your young person be organized, but leave it up to him or her to establish an application timetable and meet deadlines. Yes, the process seems confusing and is, at best, complex. Each college may have a different application deadline and request different documents. And even if a student can make sense out of these issues and fulfill all the requirements asked, he or she is not guaranteed admission.

The college admission process is best viewed as an opportunity for students to learn leadership and control as well as a time for them to move gradually from dependence to independence. If your student does not assume control or continually slips up, you can help most by not coming to the rescue! Rather than take over the process, talk through strategies with your student. Help your student learn how to address new problems as they arise. After all, once fall arrives and college registration is complete, your teen will not have a parent available at every turn or at every disappointment but will instead have to call on the problem-solving skills you have instilled to make decisions and take action.

The college decision is also a decision about familial values. Is a religious environment really best for your daughter? How important is college cost? Is it critical that your son be near relatives so he can celebrate major holidays with extended family? Would you pay more for a college you perceive as higher in status? The questions and the issues involved are endless. Most families leave their values unstated; the college decision-making process can change that. By working with your student on **Worksheets 5** and **6**, you'll find ample opportunities to discuss the values and beliefs that your family views as important.

Trust, openness, and supportiveness are key qualities that help ease the college planning process. Permit your young person to try out ideas and plans on you. Try to respond with helpful questions or suggestions rather than react in horror. It is common for students to have a different favorite college or major each week of the senior year. A student may even claim he or she is not going to go to college; often this feeling simply reflects exasperation and anxiety related to gathering information and making an important decision. Again, the best response is to provide an arena for a calm discussion of strategies. In the case of the young man who indicated he was not going to college, his mother engaged him in a discussion of the pros and cons of two alternatives—going to college or taking a year off to work.

Emotions like fear, frustration, defensiveness, and anger may arise during the college planning process. By applying to college, your young person is, perhaps for the first time, holding up his or her credentials against the light of a wider base than that provided by the home high school. And putting oneself into an entirely new level of competition often leads to fear and uncertainty. At the same time that your adolescent is making a very important decision, he or she is also deciding to leave the supportive and familiar environment of home and family. In preparing for college, a student is initiating action that causes separation and often pain. It is no surprise, then, that some students are ambivalent and procrastinate about completing their applications and, ultimately, about deciding which college to attend. Other students may feel defensive and want to be fiercely independent (gaining some early practice before leaving home). Each of these reactions is normal, human, and quite understandable. While these behaviors may tax parents' patience and tempers, empathy and understanding will go a long way toward keeping peace at home during the senior year. The year before college is one of the most poignant times for parents as they must balance their roles of separation and support. Remember, no single way of accomplishing these tasks is "best" or "right."

For a selection of resources geared to parents of high school students and college freshmen, check the "Parent Guides" section of **Appendix J, References for College Planning**. One of the best known is *Letting Go: A Parent's Guide to Understanding the College Years* by Karen L. Coburn and Madge L. Treeger. Useful information on the college admission process can be found in *The Truth About College Admission* by Barnard and Clark. Educate to Career (educatetocareer.org) provides information about the relationship between college cost and career outcomes. *Where You Go Is Not Who You'll Be* by Frank Bruni provides a current and thoughtful way to approach the college admission process. While not specifically about college, *The Paradox of Choice: Why More Is Less* by Barry Schwartz is a classic and offers valuable commentary about choices in general. College Parents (collegeparents.com) might be of interest for links to such aspects as fraternity hazing, money management, etc. For data on campus safety and security, go to ope.ed.gov/security/search.asp.

Some Specific Suggestions

The previous pages dealt with broad issues and questions. But some specific suggestions may help summarize and condense the important college planning issues for parents.

1. Assist your young person in keeping track of the college planning goals provided in **Appendices A-E.**

2. Few parents, no matter how intelligent or professionally successful, know a lot about colleges. Trust your counselor and heed his or her advice. Attend programs held at your high school concerning college planning and meet with the college counselor. While high schools vary in the help provided, you will want to take advantage of whatever resources are offered. Sometimes this means taking the initiative to ask the guidance office for assistance.

3. Encourage your son or daughter to appraise objectively his or her abilities and limitations. Consider questions such as the following. In which subjects does your young person excel? At what level are his or her high school classes? Which subjects are most difficult? How are his or her study skills? How well does he or she communicate, orally as well as on paper? What is your young person's experience in such classes as English, mathematics, laboratory sciences, foreign languages? How are his or her college entrance test scores?

4. Assist your student in assessing interests and preferences. Again, ask pertinent questions. About which subjects is your student passionate? What does he or she read for pleasure? What hobbies does he or she pursue? In which extracurricular activities has your student found the most enjoyment? Which jobs have been most interesting?

5. Help your student sort out the most important qualities in his or her choice of college (by reviewing **Worksheets 5** and **6**). As you review these qualities, you will want to arrive at consensus with your student about such issues as cost, size, distance from home, and religious affiliation. The best college decision you can help your young person make is one that represents the best match of the student's interests, abilities, preferences, and unique qualities with the characteristics and special features of any given college. The most critical consideration should be choosing an academic environment in which your young person will thrive, mature, and find enjoyment as well as stimulation.

6. Be a careful, systematic, and thoughtful aid in the information-gathering and decision-making processes. Help your student use the resources listed in **Chapter 5**. Colleges do a lot of aggressive marketing, and while students may feel flattered by receiving all their mail and phone calls, do not overinterpret the intent of the communication. But

recognize that at some point you stop gathering facts and begin gathering feelings. In other words, you need to be able to help your student see the forest through the trees. While there is a time to research specific data points (major, study abroad options, cost, campus medical facilities, etc.), there comes a time when you stop looking at specific facts and help your student weigh his or her feelings about the positives and negatives of a particular school.

7. Encourage your son or daughter to keep his or her options open and to have many college choices. Don't focus on one college too early in the process. Your son or daughter should have colleges at each level of admission selectivity. There should be at least one college where admission chances are high, one with "medium" admission chances, and one "reach" college (where admission chances are lower). Each of these colleges should be fully acceptable to you, but even more importantly, to your student. See **Chapter 5** for ways of identifying these admission categories. You can be most helpful in the application completion phase (in the fall of the senior year) by encouraging your student to establish a target date for each application and by urging systematic completion of applications (for example, complete one application per weekend for a month). **Worksheet 10** in **Chapter 5** will help keep track of application steps.

8. No college is perfect. Parents can help each student evaluate how he or she will cope with the inherent trade-offs among the good and bad features of each school.

9. Share with your student your own feelings, thoughts, and expectations about college but label them as such, i.e., your feelings, your thoughts, your expectations. Use your adult maturity and objectivity to be open-minded and nonjudgmental as you listen to your child. Avoid contributing hearsay you glean from well-meaning acquaintances or your neighbor's cousin who "knows" that College Z is "horrible."

10. Encourage your student to share his or her thoughts, feelings, and ideas about college. Talk about fears such as an admission denial, homesickness, and how you will communicate when he or she is away from home.

11. Respect your student's desires for privacy about his or her scores, grades, and other pertinent admission information. The stress and uncertainty of college planning often brings parents of students into contact with each other, and discussions about the frustrations and excitement of college planning can be beneficial. Your student's specific scores and grade point average, however, are confidential, and only he or she may choose to share them with others.

12. Be aware of the language you use as you talk to friends and extended family about college plans. Do not announce, "We are looking at small colleges" or "We've decided to attend State U." Your student is the one making the college choice; the plural pronoun, "we," is inappropriate and pulls the focus away from the central figure in the process, your student.

13. Finally, don't be tempted to think that advances in technology have made planning for college that different than it was 20 years ago. Yes, there are cell phones and Skype and instant messaging, but the uncertainty of leaving home and the need for your love remains.

Dealing with Rejection

Good college planning suggests that a student's application list should contain at least one or two "reach" schools where the likelihood of admission is slim—perhaps as low as 5-15%. Of course, as discussed in **Chapter 5**, the application list should also include a group of schools where the likelihood of admission is much higher. Given the likelihood that your son or daughter will receive some rejections, good counseling will anticipate rejection. Information on admission decisions, including wait-lists, and more thoughts about college-denial letters can be found at the end of **Chapter 8**.

Any admission denial is disappointing, and parents can help their students understand that "rejection" by a college does not mean rejection as a person. A denial usually means a college simply had too many applications for the available spaces in its dormitories or that the admission staff felt (based on their experience and judgment) the student would likely not have a successful experience there.

No matter the reasons behind it, a rejection can shatter a teenager's confidence. If expanded and repeated, rejection can do major damage to a student's sense of self-worth. The denial comes at a particularly difficult time in a teenager's life, a time when he or she is struggling with such issues as independence, confidence, and self-worth. An acceptance is seen not just as an admission to college but as admission to future success and ultimate happiness. Indeed, students may see acceptance to a prestigious university as a mark of value and worthiness. Do not let a college decision become a part of self-image—yours or your student's.

As a parent, you can help by pointing out that admission decisions are often subjective and impersonal. Be disappointed alongside your student, but do not be disappointed in your student. Decisions reflect human judgments on behalf of admission officers. For all of the information colleges have about any applicant, many bits of information remain unassessed; for example, schools cannot easily quantify or evaluate motivation, creativity, and kindness. Help your student know that regardless of the decisions made by colleges, he or she is inherently and completely worthy of being accepted.

If your student is not admitted to his or her first-choice school, recognize the feelings your young person is facing. Dealing with setbacks is never easy, but parental attitudes play a major role in a student's emotional well-being during this period. Encourage your son or daughter to bounce back and make the most of his or her available college options. Since success in college is extremely important, persuade your young person to take advantage of the opportunities available at another school. Remind him or her that getting top grades, making a real contribution to a campus community, and developing people-skills will go a long way toward employment opportunities or graduate school acceptances after four years.

If a student does receive an admission denial, parents will do well to help their student understand that such a letter is not the end of the world. Keep the process in perspective and affirm the worth of your child.

Final Comments

Parents, your role in the process of helping your young person select a college is central and important. You set the stage on which a crucial decision will take place. Your insights and your emotional level-headedness will contribute to the final choice.

Parents can help their students through the college choice process by promoting their children's self-understanding. Help them know themselves, understand their background, and recognize their values. Parents should not be expected to have vast amounts of college expertise. If finances permit, they would be wise to consult an objective outsider—a counselor—for help, advice, and experienced judgment. However, a determined parent on a budget can still ferret out information and resources to help a student through the college planning process. Above all, parents should support, respect, love, and affirm the wonderful young people they are about to help launch on their own exciting journeys.

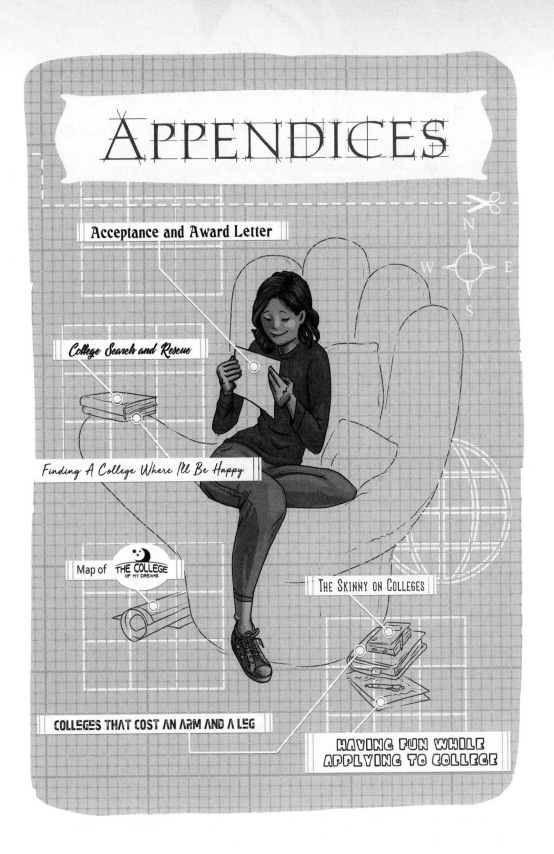

APPENDICES

Acceptance and Award Letter

College Search and Rescue

Finding A College Where I'll Be Happy

Map of THE COLLEGE OF MY DREAMS

The Skinny on Colleges

COLLEGES THAT COST AN ARM AND A LEG

HAVING FUN WHILE APPLYING TO COLLEGE

Appendix A
Eighth Grade Year—College Planning Goals

It's never too early to start planning for college. Planning early for college can set a student up for success in high school.

Essential tools. Eighth grade is the time to create strong study habits if you haven't already done so. The study habits that worked for you in middle school may not serve you well when you're faced with the rigors of a high school course load. Good study habits include limiting distractions, taking handwritten notes, and reviewing notes every day before beginning homework. Staying organized is key, so set up your own system of folders, binders, or any other method that helps you keep track of assignments, homework, and handouts. Use a calendar (paper or digital) to note and schedule all school-related tasks and activities.

Consider how you manage your time (or whether it manages you). You might find it helpful to keep a log at first so you can determine how much time you're squandering when you could be productive. It's necessary and healthy to kick back and relax, but social media, video games, and online distractions can eat up hours without you even noticing.

Academics. Your focus this year should be on doing well in school, but with an eye toward how you want to start off your high school career. Are there courses you can take in eighth grade—an advanced math class, an introduction to a foreign language—that interest you and might give you a head start in your freshman year? Just be sure that you qualify for these studies and have support from your teachers.

Extracurricular activities. Extracurriculars provide a break from studies while giving you a chance to socialize, exercise, relax, and learn. Athletes who want to play a sport in high school will want to hone their skills so they can compete at a higher level. If you're fascinated by science, participate in your school district's science fairs. History buffs can look into the National History Day competition. Follow your interests and see where they lead, be it art, dance, photography, reading, creative writing, or yes, even online pursuits in limited doses.

Use some of your free time to think about possible career interests and how they might correspond to courses you'll be taking this year and potentially in high school. No one expects you to choose a career in eighth grade, but there's a lot you can learn by exploring. Try an online search for "How to decide on a career" or talk to your parents and their friends about their work and how they chose it.

And speaking of parents, eighth grade is not too early to start family discussions about college and how to pay for it. Has your family already set aside money for college and is continuing to do so? If you have, you've got a head start on college expenses. If not, it's never too late to start building up a college fund. And it's never too early for you and your parents to think realistically about how family finances are likely to affect your choice of colleges.

Summer activities. The summer between middle school and high school can offer you an opportunity to shed habits and attitudes that you're not happy with and may have been holding you back. Depending on your family situation, your summer may involve caring for siblings or other family members, but you can still keep learning. If you need to earn money, consider starting your own business; there are lawns to be mown, gardens to be watered and weeded, older neighbors who may need errands run. If your time is your own, try out a new hobby or interest or volunteer in your community. And whatever your summer plans, do take time to recharge so you can start off your freshman year relaxed and ready to take on the challenges and rewards of high school.

Appendix B
Freshman Year—College Planning Goals

Freshman year is not just the start of a new school year but the beginning of a new learning experience. You'll have more freedom than you had in middle school but will also be expected to take on more responsibility. High school is a prelude to college but also a place where you develop as a student and as a person. To make the most of your four years, set goals for your high school career that may include honors classes, volunteer work, and extracurricular activities.

Essential tools. In order to handle the increased course load of high school, you'll need to sharpen your time management skills. Do an online search on "time management for high school students" for tips on using your time well. Track your time over the course of a week in order to identify any "time sinks" such as social media, video games, binge-watching movies or series.

Strong study habits are essential. Good study habits include limiting distractions, taking handwritten notes, and reviewing notes every day before beginning homework. Staying organized is key, so set up your own system of folders, binders, or any other method that helps you keep track of assignments, homework, and handouts. Use a calendar (paper or digital) to note and schedule all school-related tasks and activities. If you struggle with time management or staying focused, ask for help. Your teachers and counselors may be able to advise you or point you toward existing programs that may help you supercharge your studying.

Academics. This is the year that your transcript begins to be formed. The transcript is the record of all of your classes and grades and will be sent to colleges during the fall of your senior year. At the end of your freshman year, you will have completed 25% of your high school transcript.

Colleges look carefully at your grades but also consider which subject areas you studied and how rigorous your classes were. A strong college preparatory program balanced with courses in English, mathematics, social studies, science, and world languages is important. Did you opt for AP or honor classes when available and appropriate for you? The key is to push yourself yet know your limits. Your parents, teachers, and counselors may have insights into class subjects and levels that match your abilities. It's also not too early to look ahead and develop a four-year plan for high school classes. Classes that you might want to take later in your high school career may require that you have taken prerequisites (lower-level classes in the same subject area).

If you are a high school athlete aspiring to play your sport in college, become familiar with and register for the National Collegiate Athletic Association (NCAA) Clearinghouse and the National Association of Intercollegiate Athletes (NAIA) Eligibility Center. Not all high school courses count toward NCAA requirements so visit the NCAA High School Portal to verify that your school's courses are approved.

Freshman year is a great time to start expanding your word knowledge. Key to this is reading, not just assigned materials but also news media, magazines, and books. Successful college applicants are knowledgeable about a wide range of issues. In addition, a strong vocabulary will enhance your writing and help you score better on almost any test you take.

Extracurricular activities. High school offers you a wide range of activities to explore and engage in, including academic honors, clubs, sports, fine and performing arts. You may also consider out-of-school activities such as work and community service or take on a totally new challenge in an area unfamiliar to you. Whatever you decide to do with your limited free time, choose extracurriculars that align with your passions, values, strengths, and personal situation. Avoid cramming your schedule or overextending yourself so much that your grades suffer. Colleges would much rather see you dedicated to a few worthwhile endeavors than marginally involved with a bunch of clubs.

Four years is a long time to remember everything you're involved in, so maintain a record of events, successes, performances, awards, and any other significant use of your time. A great way to keep an updated list is to begin building a resume. Formats for creating a high school student resume are available on the internet. You can also use and adapt as necessary ***Worksheet 4, Activities/Experiences Record***, in this book.

College identification. No one expects you to know as a freshman which college you want to attend and what to study there. But you can start learning about the different kinds of schools and the programs they offer. Your first step is to identify sources of reliable information about colleges and universities. Not all books and websites are equally credible, and the best-selling guides or most popular sites may not be the most helpful. Explore the college planning resources available in your school, and ask your counselor or teachers if they have sources to recommend. Check out the resources listed throughout ***Chapter 5, Building Your College List***.

Even as a freshman, you can be thinking about where your passions and interests lie and how they might translate into a career. At this stage, you'll want to keep your options open and explore many possibilities. A personality assessment (widely available online) or the Self-Survey found in this book can help you identify your strengths, challenges, and communication and learning style. You can use other online assessments to determine how your strengths and interests align with potential college majors and careers. Keep in mind that the career landscape is changing all the time, so your dream job could be in a field that doesn't even exist yet!

Pay attention to what friends and others are saying about their college experiences—good and bad. Get to know your counselor as well as other school administrators who are involved in the college planning process. Building connections early in your high school career will provide you with not only a great support system, but also people who will know you well enough to write letters of recommendation.

Determine which of the standardized college entrance exams—the ACT and SAT—is right for you. Neither test is "easier" or "harder" than the other, but different types of students tend to do better on one test than the other. You can take practice tests online to see whether you score higher on the ACT or SAT. Make sure that you familiarize yourself with the most recent ACT and SAT test formats and subject areas as these may change. Some high schools will allow you to take the October PSAT as a freshman. If you can, take the PSAT or the PreACT your freshman year in order to become familiar with the test and testing protocols.

A big part of planning for college is exploring how to pay for it. **Read Chapter 4: Paying for College—Deal with It; Don't Run From It**, for information on paying for college and cost-saving strategies. Talk to your parents about funds they may have earmarked for college costs and what your family can afford to pay for college.

Summer activities. Before you dive into summer, take a moment to assess your freshman year. Did you achieve the goals you set for yourself? Do you feel good about how you managed your time? Are there skills you need to sharpen, such as writing papers or getting up to speed in a language you're studying? If you need help in any area, check with your counselor for information about free or low-cost programs that may be available in your area or online.

Keep up with your reading during the summer—news media, books, magazines—to expand your vocabulary and your view of the world. If the summer is yours to spend as you like, seek out an opportunity that allows you to explore a particular interest or an internship in a field you'd like to learn about. If you need to earn money this summer, consider whether you can turn a passion or skill into a summer job, such as math tutor or counselor at a sports camp. Athletes should start looking into and becoming familiar with NCAA and NAIA athletic recruiting requirements. As you figure out your summer plans, keep in mind that colleges like to see applicants who are motivated and interested in learning more.

Over the summer, set aside some time to research colleges and look for scholarships. Think about the characteristics of your ideal college. What size college fits you? Would you do better academically in a class of 40 or 400 students? Do you want a college that specializes in a certain subject area or one where you can explore and discover your interests? What about location? Do you need the resources and stimulation of a big city university or would you find academic success at a quieter or more isolated college? You and your parents may want to plan some informal visits to local colleges and universities just to get a feel for a college campus. Remember, you may not have been able to choose your high school, but you have lots of choices when selecting a college, so take a little time this summer to explore.

Appendix C
Sophomore Year—College Planning Goals

As you enter your sophomore year, you should by now be familiar with your school counselors and the resources of the counseling office. You probably have a sense of the courses that will challenge you and those that are just transcript filler. You have joined clubs or participated in other activities outside the classroom and may be considering some new ones to try as a sophomore.

Essential tools. As you look back on your freshman year, consider whether you met your goals and consistently did your best work. If you haven't performed up to your potential, think about areas that could be improved, such as time management or study habits. Do you keep distractions at a minimum, keep notes in class, and review your notes daily before beginning homework? If you feel like you're drowning in papers and can't keep track of assignments, homework, and handouts, set up your own system of folders, binders, or any method that works for you. Use a calendar (paper or digital) to note and schedule all school-related tasks and activities.

Work on your ability to read and retain information. Does you vocabulary proficiency need a boost? As you consume news media and read journals, note and learn words that you're unfamiliar with. Various tools to boost your vocabulary are available online. Assess your writing strengths and weaknesses; ask your teachers for suggestions or look online for ideas to improve your writing. Save important projects and copies of your best writing. They can be tools when you're writing a resume or helpful reminders to jog the memory of teachers who are writing your letters of recommendation.

To better plan your classes, investigate possible college majors and careers and how your high school curriculum relates to these areas. Think about what interests you and how those interests might translate into career paths. Keep your mind open, and investigate lots of possibilities.

Academics. Stay focused on keeping your grades up. If your GPA isn't where you want it to be, get help with study strategies from your teachers. Your high school transcript—the record of all your courses and grades—is part of your application that will be sent to colleges in the fall of your senior year. At that time, grades from your first semester of your senior high school year likely won't be available. This means that when college admission officers review your transcript, they'll be paying close attention to your junior and sophomore grades. By the end of sophomore year, 50% of your transcript will be set in stone.

Colleges will look carefully at your classes (and not just your grades). A strong college preparatory program balanced with courses in English, mathematics, social studies, science, and languages is important to prepare yourself for the rigors of college. If your school offers higher-level (honors or AP) classes, consider whether these are right for you. You should be taking the highest level of academics that you can handle without overly stressing. Your teachers or counselor can provide insights into whether your course load is appropriate. It's not too early to plan for courses you may want to take in your junior and senior years. Keep in mind that courses you may want to take as a junior or senior could require prerequisites (lower-level classes in the same subject area).

If you are a high school athlete aspiring to play your sport in college, become familiar with and register for the National Collegiate Athletic Association (NCAA) Clearinghouse and the National Association of Intercollegiate Athletes (NAIA) Eligibility Center. Not all high school courses count toward NCAA requirements; you can find out if your school's courses are approved at the NCAA High School Portal.

Consider which teachers you would ask to write your college recommendations. Although some colleges require letters of recommendation from junior and senior year only, most allow teachers from any high school year to write recommendation letters.

Extracurricular activities. As a sophomore, you may already be participating in a range of non-academic extracurricular activities. See if you can deepen your involvement or take on a leadership role in a club or team in which you currently participate. You also might want to consider stepping outside your comfort zone and trying something new.

Maintain a record of events, successes, performances, awards, and other significant uses of your time. A great way to keep an updated list is to build a resume. Formats for creating a high school student resume are available on the internet. You can also use and adapt as necessary **Worksheet 4, Activities/Experiences Record**, in this book.

College identification. Meet with your school counselor at least once this year to discuss your course selection and other college planning matters. Consider the college counseling office a resource for answers to your questions about new courses and suggestions for ways to develop your interests. Find out how college planning operates at your school. Does your school use an online platform like Naviance or Scior? If so, become familiar with using it. Ask your counselor what you should do this year to prepare for college. If you're an athlete who aspires to play your sport in college, inform your counselor that you are considering college athletics.

This may the year that you take the PSAT or PreAct. Determine which of the standardized college entrance exams—the ACT and SAT—is right for you. Neither test is "easier" or "harder" than the other, but different types of students tend to do better on one test than the other. You can take practice tests online to determine whether you score higher on the

ACT or SAT. Make sure that you familiarize yourself with the most recent ACT and SAT test formats and subject areas as these may change. The PSAT is also the National Merit Scholarship Qualifying Test, so if you are interested in National Merit Scholarships, you must take this test. Even if you do not need merit aid, taking the PSAT is terrific practice for the SAT and will give you a general idea of how well you will perform on the SAT as well as familiarity with SAT testing protocols and content.

Sophomore year is an ideal time to jumpstart your college research. Think about those qualities that would make a college right for you. What size is best? Do you have location preferences? What is your preferred college culture? To zero in on what really matters to you, complete **Worksheet 5, Qualities That Will Make a College Right for You**.

Continue to pay attention to reliable and trusted sources of college information, including websites, books, and colleges themselves. Attend meetings with the college representatives who visit your school, even if you think you're not interested in that particular school; you're sure to learn about the college application process and you may just find a college you like. If you request information from colleges, be sure that the email address you provide for college material is one that you check often. And remember that getting email, mail, or texts from colleges doesn't mean you will get in.

Pay attention to what friends and others are saying about their college experiences. Quiz college students that you know about their experiences. "Why did you pick this college?" "What do you like best?" "Least?" If possible, visit some college campuses and take note of positive and negative features. Attend local college and career fairs to meet representatives and gather information.

Family finances can change over time so keep talking with your parents about paying for a college education. Check your school's counseling office for scholarship information, and look at online resources about financial aid to see whether you would qualify. Don't forget to research the numerous merit scholarships that may be available to you not only from the colleges themselves but also from corporations and civic organizations or because of your ancestry, ethnicity, intended field of study, or athletic participation. Your parents will want to continue researching how to pay for college and set up a college budget. Both you and your parents should pay attention to **Chapter 4** of this book, **Paying for College.**

If you're an athlete intending to play at the college level, double-check that your classes meet the NCAA Clearinghouse requirements. Use the NCAA Eligibility Center's High School Portal to see whether your school's courses are NCAA-approved. This is the right time to begin to create your sports resume and recruitment videos. You will want to find the names of coaches at colleges of interest and follow instructions at each college about ways of demonstrating your interest.

Summer activities. As your sophomore year comes to a close, consider how the year went. Did you achieve the goals you set for yourself? Do you feel good about how you managed your time? Are there skills you need to sharpen, such as writing papers or getting up to speed in a language you're studying? If you need help in any of these area, check with your counselor for ideas or search the internet for free or low-cost programs that may be available in your local area or online.

Create a summer plan for test preparation, taking a low-key approach toward getting ready for the SAT and ACT. You could set aside a certain number of hours per week for test prep, using some of the test preparation programs available on line at no cost. If you think you'd like a more directed program, a prep course or private study could be a worthwhile investment of your summer time.

If you plan to work this summer, try to find a job in a field or business area that interests you. No matter where you end up working, learn as much as you can, whether it's food service, camp counseling, or your own lawn-mowing business. If you are free to make your own summer plans, continue exploring your interests through travel, an internship, volunteering, self-designed project, or other learning experiences.

Try to think broadly and creatively about ways to use your summer. In the college admissions officer's eyes, summer vacation matters because it provides insight into how you choose to spend your free time. Colleges love to see applicants who are motivated and interested in learning more. You can demonstrate your motivation and interest in learning whether you're tackling a new hobby or interest, caring for a sibling or other family members, participating in a specialized high school program, taking a college class or free course online, volunteering in your community, or creating your own internship.

Appendix D
Junior Year—College Planning Goals

Junior year is the year when lots of students suddenly realize that college is on the horizon. If you're someone who hasn't been thinking much about college, it's not too late to start. Even if you haven't actively looked at college options and careers, you probably have taken a range of classes and participated in a variety of extracurricular activities, knowing that these will impact your admission to college. But whether you're late to the college search or have been thinking about colleges since middle school, your junior year is an important one.

Essential tools. Take a moment to look back on your freshman and sophomore years. Did you meet your academic goals, consistently do your best work, and improve in areas where you were lagging behind? If you feel you haven't performed up to your potential, where could you improve? Your junior year course load may be intense so it's essential to sharpen your time management and study habits. Have a system in place to track assignments, homework, and handouts, using folders, binders, or any method that works for you. Use a calendar (paper or digital) to note and schedule all school-related tasks and activities.

Work on your ability to read and retain information. Does you vocabulary proficiency need a boost? As you consume news media and read journals, note and learn any words that you're unfamiliar with. Various tools to boost your vocabulary are available online. Assess your writing strengths and weaknesses; ask your teachers for suggestions or look online for ways to improve your writing. Keep copies of your best writing and important projects. These can be helpful as you maintain your resume and start working on college essays. You might even give copies of your writing to teachers who you want to know more about you, especially any teacher who may be writing your recommendation letters.

Academics. Good grades count! By the end of junior year, 75% of your transcript will complete, so keep your grades up. This is key because your junior year grades are the last ones that some colleges will see before making admission decisions. When colleges review your transcripts, they will look closely at your sophomore and junior year grades, so it pays off to work hard this year.

Colleges carefully consider not only your grades but also your classes. By this point in their high school careers, many college-hound students are taking a balanced college preparatory program with courses in English, mathematics, social studies, science, and languages. Whatever classes you take should be at the highest academic level that you can handle. The key is to push yourself, but know your limits. Consult with your teachers or counselor about the availability of honors, AP, or IB classes and whether they are right for you.

To better plan your classes, investigate possible college majors and careers and how your high school curriculum relates to these areas. Think about your interests and how those they might translate into career paths. Keep your mind open, and investigate lots of possibilities. As you look toward to your senior year of high school, plan your course load carefully and register for senior year classes as soon as feasible. Most colleges look carefully at the breadth and depth of your senior schedule and want to see a strong senior year course load, including five academic classes.

Extracurricular activities. Continue with your extracurricular activities with an eye toward showing colleges not only your commitment but also your skills. Are you a leader, a dedicated volunteer, a star performer, a team player, a behind-the-scenes tech wizard? Take time to update your activity record, adding any new interests or involvements. Spend time working on a resume that lists all your activities, both inside and outside the classroom. An online search for examples of a high school student resume can provide some formats to follow. You can also use and adapt as necessary *Worksheet 3, Activities/Experiences Record*, in this book.

College identification. Set up a study schedule to prepare for college entrance exams. Test prep for the SAT and ACT—on your own, in a course, or with tutoring—will pay off. The amount of time you'll need to devote to test prep will depend on your starting scores on a sample test and the average scores at your top college choices. As you prepare for these exams, be consistent in your studying and keep distractions to a minimum. If you take any of the SAT and ACT practice tests available on line, try to simulate testing conditions. Stick to time limits and refrain from looking up answers. You'll be better prepared to take the actual exams if you have studied and practiced ahead of time.

Your test prep schedule should take into account testing dates. High school juniors take the PSAT/NSMQT (Preliminary SAT/National Merit Scholarship Qualifying Test) in October. Even if you are not looking for merit aid, the PSAT is helpful as an introduction to the SAT. It also provides a general idea of how well you will perform on the SAT as well as familiarity with SAT testing protocols and content. As a junior, you can also take the ACT as early as September and the SAT as early as October. Mostly likely you will take your first ACT or SAT test between December and May of this junior year. Colleges accept both the SAT and the ACT; choose the test that you scored highest on in your practice tests. After taking any college entrance exam, if you are dissatisfied with your scores, you can retake the test and see if your scores improve. The colleges you apply to will look at your highest scores.

As a junior, you'll be getting serious about finding a college that's right for you. Look for reliable sources of information (many are listed in *Chapter 5, Building Your College List*) and don't obsess about college rankings or the schools your friends are applying to. You are looking for schools (note the plural) that fit you and offer what you want in a college. Being organized will make your college search and planning easier to handle. Set up a "College

Planning" folder (either a paper one or on your desktop) for all documents related to your college search. Start or continue your college search by attending a local college fair and presentations by college admission representatives if they are offered at your high school.

Think about what you want in your prospective college. Research is a must, so read extensively, use your school counseling office, and check out guidebooks, videos, and websites. You can also gather information from friends, teachers, current college students, and your parents. Once you've created a preliminary list of colleges, narrow your choices using your preferences in terms of location, size of the school, cost, student characteristics, academic program of study and majors offered, and financial aid availability. Don't narrow your list too much, however! You want to still have a number of acceptances and at least two financial aid safety schools.

Depending on your family's finances, you will want to keep financial planning on your radar as you do your college research. Ask your counselor about financial aid and potential merit scholarships. On your own, conduct a web search to uncover scholarships and merit aid available to you not only from various colleges but also from corporations and civic organizations on the basis of your ancestry, ethnicity, intended field of study, or athletic participation.

Schedule a meeting with your school counselor to ask questions about college choices, your senior year schedule, testing, and anything else you're curious about. Find out how college planning operates at your school; identify resources available to you. Does your school use an online platform like Naviance or Scior? If so, get familiar with using it. Let your counselor know which colleges you're considering and ask for any additional suggestions. Ask about potential merit scholarships and schools with good financial aid. Continue to develop your relationship with your counselor; he or she is typically asked to write a recommendation for you.

Share your college preferences with your teachers, and ask if they can point you toward other colleges that might be a good fit. Although you may ultimately need only one or two teacher recommendations, identify and informally talk to three teachers about writing a letter of recommendation for you.

If you're an athlete intending to play at the college level, you should complete online athletic recruitment forms for each college you're considering. You'll find these on the college's website under "athletics." Double-check that your classes meet the NCAA Clearinghouse requirements. Use the NCAA Eligibility Center's High School Portal to see whether your school's courses are NCAA-approved. After completing all online recruitment forms and ensuring your courses meet NCAA requirements, create your sports resume and recruitment videos. Send these materials to college coaches, and fill out the athletic recruitment surveys on the college websites.

If you are a performing or visual artist or interested in either these fields or graphic design, film, and related disciplines, take time to explore how the audition and portfolio processes work in college admission. Sign up to attend Performing and Visual Arts (PVA) College Fairs. Create a spreadsheet to help you keep track of admissions requirements for any fine and performing arts programs you are considering. Be sure you check the requirements for each individual college to determine what you need to submit with regard to a portfolio of your work or audition materials.

If possible, start to visit some of the colleges that rose to the top of your college match searches. Even if you're not interested in a college close to home, check out colleges within driving distance if only to see examples of different types of schools such as single-sex, small liberal arts, larger university, etc. With your parents, discuss your college choices and any financial considerations that would affect your college options, such as availability of aid, travel costs, and other expenses. Have a family meeting to block out dates for college visits throughout junior year.

Summer activities. College admission officers look at your summer activities to see how you choose to spend your time outside of school. If you need to work, either at a job or caring for siblings or other family members, consider how you can turn this into a learning experience. Check the counseling office for information on possible paid internships. If earning money is not a concern, consider volunteer work or research in a field that interests you.

Do spend time this summer to refine and finalize your college list. Be sure it reflects a balance of admission probabilities (likely, possible, and reach schools). Research the type of applications required for each school on your list, as these vary, and determine whether an interview is offered or required. Create a spreadsheet of requirements, interview information, and all deadlines for each college. Request information from colleges to demonstrate your interest and get on their radar. Remember to use an e-mail account that you check frequently.

Complete the Common Application and/or other generic and individual college applications. Write a draft personal statement for the Common Application and work on essays for the schools that require them. Organize and update your high school resume and list of extracurricular activities. If possible, continue to visit colleges on your list and consider a road trip with your parents to any schools that may be within a few hours' drive.

If you think summer is too early to begin working on your application, consider that your senior year is likely to be your busiest, with your most demanding course load and intensive extracurriculars. Your goal should be to have all your college applications completed by November 1 of your senior year. The more you can complete over the summer, the less stress you'll feel in the fall.

Appendix E
Senior Year—College Planning Goals

You're in the home stretch of your high school career! At this point, your college list of five to ten schools should be finalized (or nearly so) and your academic record and extracurricular resume almost complete. Still, you'll want to keep your grades up and maintain your activities. Do your best to keep college application drama to a minimum with your friends and family, and take time to enjoy your senior year.

Essential tools. Now, more than ever, you need to be well organized and managing your time efficiently. In addition to handling your senior year academic course load and extracurricular activities, you'll need to keep track of and meet college application deadlines and requirements. You may want to create a two-track system (digital or manual)—one to organize all school-related material for your senior year, the other for all matters related to your college search and application process. Use each track to note important dates and deadlines; store essays, assignments and other materials; and generally stay on top of all you have to do. Many students use a separate file folder for every college they're applying to. If you are filing for financial aid, you will want to pay close attention to deadlines for filing the Free Application for Federal Student Aid (FAFSA) and the CSS Profile (if required). No matter what organizing system you choose, work on your applications steadily and systematically.

Academics. It's important to keep your grades up. Remember, many colleges will be looking at your first semester grades to see whether you've taken competitive courses and received good grades. Keep your best writing and projects from this first semester. You may want to include them in your college applications, if applicable.

Extracurricular activities. Continue pursuing and contributing to your clubs, teams, volunteer work, and other activities. Update your activity resume with any awards, commendations, or recognition that could be included in your college applications.

College identification. Focus on your applications, even if your college list isn't quite finalized. College applications vary with every school, but many have similar prompts and your draft essays may be amended to fit. If possible, avoid formulaic writing. Have a good time with the essay, and don't be afraid to demonstrate your individuality. If you know someone who writes well and whose opinions you trust, ask that person to review your essay. Before sending any essay to a college, proofread it once, twice, three times. The essay is an essential part of the application process, so make sure you're proud of what you've written.

Review your college list one more time. You may find it helpful to list the pros and cons of each school you're considering. Your time is limited, and it's better to jettison a school where you won't be happy than expend hours, energy, and money on an application. Early in your senior year, schedule a meeting with your school counselor to get feedback on your final college list, review application deadlines, and ask any questions you may have.

Provide your school administration or counseling office with the list of the school to which you are applying and all deadlines for sending transcripts, letters of recommendation, and any other materials that must be provided directly by your high school. Make sure that the school administration and counseling office have everything they need from you. If you feel that due to circumstances or better preparation you could improve your college entrance exam test scores, retake the SAT or ACT.

Don't delay in deciding which teachers, counselors, coaches, or other adults in your life (your employer, volunteer supervisor, etc.) you want to write your recommendation letters. Remember that other students are also soliciting letters from these adults. Make a formal request and ask what materials or information they need from you. Provide them with a firm deadline by which the letters must be submitted to the colleges.

Visit your school's counseling office for information about financial aid. Investigate any relevant scholarship possibilities and merit aid that you may be eligible to receive. Don't overlook local scholarships or those provided by corporations and civic organizations on the basis of your ancestry, ethnicity, intended field of study, or athletic participation. Standardized forms (the FAFSA, for example) are available after October 1.

If you are applying for federal financial aid, you will need to submit the Free Application for Federal Student Aid (FAFSA) every college year in order to qualify to grants, scholarships, federal work-study, and federal student loans. Deadlines vary for federal, state, and institutional aid. The FAFSA open date for the upcoming school year (your freshman year of college) is October 1 of your senior high school year. To improve your chances of qualifying for aid, you should file your FAFSA as close to the FAFSA open date as possible. The deadline for submitting your FAFSA is June 30 after the school year for which aid is needed, i.e., June 30 of your freshman year in college. However, to meet financial aid deadlines for your state and college and obtain aid dollars in time for the start of college, you must submit the form much earlier. In addition, certain kinds of aid, such as federal work-study money and many state and institutional grants, are awarded to students who apply the earliest.

Talk with your school counselor and parents about the pros and cons of applying early decision or early action. Be aware that you can only apply early decision to one college, and if accepted, you are expected to attend. (Early action applications aren't as stringent, but fewer colleges offer this option.) Early decision notification dates are around mid-December for most schools, and if you are rejected, you may have a limited window in which to apply to other schools. However, if you are confident about your first-choice college and your chances of getting admitted, applying early can make sense. You'll know where you'll be next year and can breathe a sigh of by mid-December. Deadlines for early decision applications range from about November 1 to December 15 of your senior year, but to ensure materials arrive on time, submit your ED or EA applications no later than late October.

Deadlines for regular decision at many colleges are typically around January 1. However, some universities require submission by December 1 if you want to be considered for scholarship opportunities. Students interested in the arts should be aware that many portfolio-based arts programs have early deadlines as well. Whether or not these early deadlines apply to you, your best bet is to work diligently to complete and submit all regular decision applications no later than mid-December. Better yet, you'll feel a lot more thankful over Thanksgiving break if you complete all your applications before November 15.

Make meeting deadlines a priority. If you have any questions or concerns about materials required, deadlines, or any other aspect of the application, email the college directly.

Once your applications are received, you may have the opportunity to interview with a college representative. This interview could take place on campus if the college is located nearby. If the college is out of state or hours away, the interview might be conducted virtually and/or be with a local alumna/alumnus. You should prepare for any college interview as you might for a job interview. Even for a virtual interview, dress as you would for an important school event. You should be able to clearly state your interest in this particular college as opposed to other schools. Practice with a family member or friend, and be sure you have your facts straight. For example, you don't want to mention a basketball championship that was never won or a famous professor who teacher at a different school.

As noted previously, most colleges notify early decision and early action applicants around December 15. If you are rejected as an ED or EA applicant, you have a two-week window to apply to some colleges. Fortunately, many other schools have later application deadlines, even through August. However, the longer you wait to apply, the more limited your choices will be.

If you apply regular decision, colleges have until April 1 to release decisions, but you can expect to hear from schools starting in mid-March. If you are waitlisted and want to pursue admission to one or more colleges, don't give up hope. Let the college know immediately that you're still excited and ready to attend. Send updated grades, extracurricular information, and any new honors to boost your chances. Check your email regularly for waitlist notifications.

You're accepted!! What now? If you have colleges to choose from, first check the deadline by which you must accept or reject the offer. For most schools, the date is May 1, but colleges may have different deadlines. If you fail to accept the offer by the deadline, you will lose your place. Whether you are rejecting or accepting admission, be sure to let every college know your decision. You should also keep your high school counseling office informed of your admission decisions.

Look over your acceptances and reevaluate. Which school aligns most closely with your core values, intended career path, and qualities you want in a college? Compare financial aid packages. Let the college know immediately if there have been any recent changes to your family's income, such as a parent making a job or career change; this information could affect your aid package. Try not to be influenced by where your friends are going. College is a place to move on and grow, not relive your high school experience.

Once you've made your decision, return your signed acceptance letter and student/parent loan applications to your college. If you will be living on campus, make sure you meet housing deadlines and send in your housing deposit. Other fees, including tuition, may also be due at this time. Many schools offer flexible payment plans, so look into these if you need them.

And don't forget one final item on your college admission to-do list. Take time to thank the people who provided recommendations or other assistance during your college search and tell them which school you'll be attending. Depending on the individual and how close your relationship, you can do this in person, by phone, or via correspondence.

Summer activities. Learn everything you can about your chosen college: facilities, support services, travel options to campus, requirements for your degree, how to find your advisor, etc. Try to attend a summer orientation program at your school to familiarize yourself with the campus. If possible, arrange a meeting with an academic advisor at your college to plan your classes. Set up a bank account on or near campus.

Find out what you need in terms of college purchases—for your dorm, your classes, etc. Communicate with your new roommate(s) so you won't be complete strangers when you meet in person and to avoid duplicating any room items that can be shared.

If you have summer employment, make sure your employer know where you'll be attending and when you need to be on campus. Keep saving for college and continue to apply for scholarships; you'll be paying for college for the next four years.

Appendix F
Possible Major Fields of Study

Arts

PERFORMING ARTS
Acting
Ballet
Dance
Music
Theater arts
FINE ARTS
Animation and special
   effects
Architecture
Ceramics

Clothing and textiles studies
Creative writing
Culinary arts
Digital arts
Fashion design
Film studies
Furniture design and
   manufacturing
Game and interactive media
   design
Graphic design

Illustration
Interior design
Metal and jewelry arts
Musicology/
   ethnomusicology
Photography
Sculpture
Studio arts
Web design

Business

Accounting
Actuarial science
Advertising
Construction management
E-commerce
Economics
Entrepreneurship

Finance
General business
Healthcare administration/
   management
Hospitality management
Human resources
   management

Insurance
Management science
Marketing
Organizational studies
Real estate
Supply chain management
Tourism

Education

Art education
Child and family studies
Elementary education

Health education
Music education
Physical education

Secondary education
Special education

Engineering

Aerospace
Agricultural
Architectural
Biomedical
Chemical
Civil
Computer

Electrical
Environmental
Industrial
Marine
Mechanical
Nuclear
Petroleum

Plastics/polymer
Software
Structural
Telecommunications
Water resources

Humanities

Area/ethnic studies	Drama	Linguistics
Art and/or music history	English	Literature
Classics	Ethics	Music
Comparative literature	Foreign languages	Philosophy
Cultural and race studies	Gender studies	Religious studies/theology

Languages and Cultural Studies

Africana studies	Gay and lesbian studies/	Linguistics
American Indian/Native	transgender/queer studies	Native American
American	Gender studies	Near and middle eastern
Ancient Greek	German	Norwegian
Arabic	Hebrew	Polish
Asian	Hindi	Portuguese
Black studies	Hispanic/Latino/a studies	Religious studies
Buddhist	Iranian	Russian
Celtic	Irish	Slavic
Classics	Islamic	Spanish
Danish	Italian	Swedish
Dutch	Japanese	Theology
Filipino/Tagalog	Judaic	Turkish
French	Korean	Ukrainian
	Latin	Women's studies

Public Administration/Politics/Law

International relations	Public administration	Public health
Legal studies	Urban development	Public policy
Political science	Government	

Occupational Studies

Actuarial science	Exercise science	Medical assistant
Agriculture	Fashion design	Medical technology
Air traffic control	Fire science	Nursing
Aviation	Golf course operation and	Nutrition
Broadcasting	grounds management	Occupational therapy
Chef/culinary arts	Health and wellness	Paralegal studies
City planning	Health sciences	Paramedic
Computer and electronics	Homeland security	Pharmacology
careers	HVAC technician	Physical therapy
Construction trades	Journalism	Pilot
Criminal justice/criminology	Landscape designer	Plumber
Dental hygiene	Law enforcement	Protection services (police,
Driving occupations	Library and information	fire, etc.)
(delivery, ride share, etc.)	science	Radiation therapist
Electrician	Mechanics and repairs	Recreation and leisure studies
Equestrian studies	Media studies	Speech pathology

Urban planning

Veterinary technology

Video game design/digital arts/ multimedia

Web developer

Science and Mathematics

Artificial intelligence

Astronomy

Atmospheric sciences and meteorology

Biochemistry

Biology

Biotechnology

Botany

Chemistry

Computer and information sciences

Computer science

Crop science

Earth science

Ecology

Environmental science

Exercise science

Food science

Forensic science

Forestry

Genetics

Geology

Information science

Management information systems

Marine biology

Materials science

Mathematics

Meteorology

Neuroscience

Nutrition sciences

Nutrition/nutrition sciences

Operations management

Organic chemistry

Packaging science

Pathology

Pharmacology

Physics

Physiology

Statistics

Sustainability studies

Water quality and wastewater treatment

Wildlife management

Zoology

Social Sciences/Social Studies

Anthropology

Archaeology

Art history

Cognitive science

Communication studies

Criminology

Economics

Ethics

Gender studies

Geography

History

Human communication Studies

Law

Peace and conflict studies

Philosophy

Politics/Political science

Psychology

Religious Studies

Sociology

* Remember that this is a sampling of potential college majors. There is a wide variety of ways colleges name particular areas of study. If a college doesn't have a specific major as described here, tell the college what you want to study and see if there are courses that meet your needs. Some of the majors listed might be more typically studied on the graduate (and, hence, not on the undergraduate) level. That is, more specific majors (such as 'gender studies') might be studied in graduate school after you have a solid grounding in fields such as sociology and psychology. While getting prepared for a particular career may be one of your goals in college, remember that it is common for students to change their major. Also, be aware that general majors such as English, political science, history, and psychology provide good preparation for lots of different careers. Also, note that most students take more courses *outside* of their major compared to the number of courses taken *in* ones major. Also, note there is a distinction between "field of study" and "career." Students choose a field of study based on their interests when they are in high school. Careers are chosen after a student has taken a variety of classes in college and learns more about specific vocational options.

Appendix G
Potential College Activities List

Check those involvements that have some interest to you.

_____ Academic clubs/organizations such as English Society, Business Student Association, Pre-Med Society, Political Science Association, American Society of Civil Engineers, Computer Club, Robotics Club, Astronomy Club

_____ Admission office assistance such as giving tours, contacting prospective students, developing admission policies

_____ Affinity groups such as LGBTQ Center, survivors of domestic/sexual abuse, Black Student Union, Feminist Coalition, South Asian Student Alliance, Animal Rights Club, Women in STEM

_____ Athletics/sports/recreation such as varsity, club and intramural sports, bicycling, outdoor adventurers, sailing, ultimate Frisbee, climbing club, floor hockey, Quidditch club

_____ Debate/forensics/public speaking

_____ Environmental groups such as Greenpeace, Rain Forest Action group, Global Change Action group, Green Residence Hall, A Cleaner Tomorrow

_____ Fraternity/sorority (Greek organizations)

_____ Government such as residence hall judiciary board, various leadership councils and advisory committees, student senate

_____ International student organizations/multicultural group such as Arab, Italian American, Vietnamese, Latino Student Organization, Model UN

_____ Job on-campus such as research assistant, data analyst, teacher assistants, graders, lab assistants

_____ Job off campus such as work in near campus stores and restaurants.

_____ Journalism/communication such as newspaper, yearbook, literary magazines, radio stations, television stations, other campus publications

_____ Musical activity such as choir, jazz ensemble, marching band, rock band, chamber orchestra

_____ Performing arts such as drama, dance, visual arts, improv club, comedy club, reenactment clubs (including revolutionary war reenactments or LARPing)

_____ Religious group, including Sikh Student Association, Jewish Student Union, Fellowship of Christian Athletes

_____ Reserve Officers' Training Corps (ROTC)

_____ Social/political action groups such as Global Action Against Poverty, College Democrats or Republicans, United Students Against Sweatshops, drug or alcohol awareness, Amnesty International, Habitat for Humanity, Students for Global Health

_____ Student center activity such as planning for speakers, exhibits, concerts

Appendix H
College Planning Values Assessment

Name: _____

Students have different reasons for going to college. Defining your values is an essential first step in identifying the colleges where you will fit in and be happy.

What do you want college to do for you? Here are 12 suggested reasons why you might want to attend college.

1. To learn about different cultures, peoples, backgrounds, etc.
2. To expand my potential lifetime earnings
3. To learn essential life skills so that I can be a better parent and citizen
4. To find a vocational direction in life
5. To gain more independence and a greater sense of freedom
6. To create long-lasting relationships and professional connections
7. To have a fresh start where no one knows me
8. To gain new skills and experiences
9. To enable me to receive a degree from a high-quality school
10. To explore the U.S. and perhaps the world
11. To take advantage of college life: spectator sports, clubs, activities, etc.
12. To get the best education possible at a reasonable cost

To complete this assessment, you will consider these 12 values and record how important the value is to you on a scale from "a most important reason" to "a least important reason."

There are no "right" answers here. Every student will have a different response to these values. Although several, or even most, of these values may be significant for you in one way or another, the goal (as you will see below) is to decide which three are the most important.

Here are the 12 values:

1. To learn about different cultures, peoples, backgrounds, etc.
People vary in terms of gender, socioeconomic background, religious background, cultural background, and more. We differ from one another regarding what kind of music we like, how we want to spend a Saturday afternoon, and what type of food we eat. In your classes, in the residence hall, and all across campus, you will encounter diversity of all sorts. Coming face to face with diversity helps us see that the little bubble that we come from is but one of many such bubbles that exist worldwide.

Students are exposed to all kinds of ideas in college, and you will often run into situations in which beliefs don't line up with one another. You will encounter instances where your really-smart-seeming professor wholly disagrees with the ideas of another really-smart-seeming professor. Learning how to work with and assess a variety of ideas is an important goal of any college education.

1. How important is "to learn about different cultures, peoples, etc." as a reason for my going to college?

Most Important Reason	Important Reason	Indifferent	Unimportant Reason	Least Important Reason

2. To expand my potential lifetime earnings
More money! Yes, college graduates make, on average, thousands of dollars more a year than do those who didn't earn a college degree. Over a lifetime of earnings, this difference amounts to hundreds of thousands of dollars. You will want to think about earning potential, advancement opportunities, and the future market for the careers you consider. You will want to consider this value in your career planning.

Remember, however, that there is no sure road to riches! You not only must pick a career direction carefully but also choose a college where the potential for academic success is high. When it comes to securing a good job or being admitted to graduate school, the name of a particular college is less important than your GPA or contributions to campus life. Even if you find that a particular career has tremendous earning potential, those earnings may come to only those who are most successful in the profession. Look at the average salaries and consider your interests, values, and personality before making your final career choice. Be sure to take advantage of hands-on learning opportunities such as internships that interest you and could give you insight into different occupations. In addition, finding good, career-focused summer jobs can be helpful in determining what fields align with your interests, abilities, and goals.

2. How important is "to expand my potential lifetime earnings" as a reason for my going to college?

Most Important Reason	Important Reason	Indifferent	Unimportant Reason	Least Important Reason

3. To learn essential life skills so that I can be a better parent and citizen
College life puts you into a community that can serve as a prototype to a more informed life post-college. College gives you the chance to reflect on your values and character and develop a deeper and broader understanding of social issues. Playing an active role on a college campus can foster civic participation over a lifetime. Intellectual discussion can provide you with critiquing, debate, and discussion skills. Facts learned in the classroom

about subjects such as history, psychology, business, etc., could provide information you need to answer questions posed by children and ultimately lead to better parenting. If religion and/or spirituality are important to you, college may provide insights that will be helpful in community or family life.

3. How important is "to learn essential life skills to be a better parent and citizen" as a reason for my going to college?

Most Important Reason	Important Reason	Indifferent	Unimportant Reason	Least Important Reason

4. To find a vocational direction in life

Finding a career that will be fulfilling is one of the most critical choices you will make in your life. Your selection of a college will be your first step toward achieving your career goal. If you have tentatively selected a career, college will allow you to take courses leading to a degree in your chosen field. If you don't yet know what job would suit you, remember that a broad, solid liberal arts foundation is considered good preparation for most professions. College offers you an opportunity to explore different options and areas of interest. You will want to look at opportunities for internships and take advantage of the career planning and placement office at your chosen college. Most schools don't require students to declare a major until the end of their sophomore year. That gives you two years to work on general courses and explore different majors.

4. How important is "to find a vocational direction in life" as a reason for my going to college?

Most Important Reason	Important Reason	Indifferent	Unimportant Reason	Least Important Reason

5. To gain more independence and a greater sense of freedom

Gaining personal autonomy is vital to many young people. College is, in general, a time for independence, and students are often eager to make their own decisions without parental involvement. If you feel you can handle a high level of autonomy, you will want to look for colleges where there is some freedom in choosing courses and where students are given responsibility for their own lives. If you consider independence a priority, you may want to think carefully about where and how that independence will be cultivated. Some students find a great sense of autonomy when they are farther from home. Others may want to reach an agreement with parents about how much contact is suitable for the level of independence desired.

5. How important is "to gain more independence and a greater sense of freedom" as a reason for my going to college?

Most Important Reason	Important Reason	Indifferent	Unimportant Reason	Least Important Reason

6. To create long-lasting relationships and professional connections

The college years are a time to make lifelong friends as well as develop relationships with professors and other adults who are authorities and experts in their fields. Given the diversity often found on college campuses, the odds are good you will find people as like you and unlike you as possible, and some of them may become friends for life. If building these kinds of relationships is important to you, consider carefully the composition of the student body at colleges of interest. Where will the friendships you seek be most likely to be created and sustained?

6. How important is "to gain more independence and a greater sense of freedom"' as a reason for my going to college?

Most Important Reason	Important Reason	Indifferent	Unimportant Reason	Least Important Reason

7. To have a fresh start where no one knows me

For the most part, you arrive at college as a blank slate. You can hang out with a different group of people or be a completely different person. Some students who may have been quiet to a fault in high school make a conscious effort to open up in college. Students who didn't have tons of friends in high school may prioritize widening their social circle of friends or developing deeper relationships in college. Expectations play a role in the person we are in high school, where students are readily characterized as "nerds" or "jocks" or known primarily for being musicians or actors. Sometimes these labels become indelible, and some students feel they can't shake the expectations others have of them. All that changes in college where a "new you" is possible.

7. How important is "to have a fresh start where no one knows me" as a reason for my going to college?

Most Important Reason	Important Reason	Indifferent	Unimportant Reason	Least Important Reason

8. To gain new skills and experiences

College is all about growing, personally and professionally. "Newness"" is an experience everyone has in college—often every day! New classes, new activities, new milieu. You may envision college as an adventure and will want to pick schools where you can meet your need for stimulation and excitement. Because you value newness, you should not hesitate to attend college in a different part of the country or experience an environment or an entirely different climate from your high school.

8. How important is "to gain new skills and experiences" as a reason for my going to college?

Most Important Reason	Important Reason	Indifferent	Unimportant Reason	Least Important Reason

9. To receive a degree from a high-quality school

For students who are intellectually focused or academically strong, attaining a high-quality college education may be a long-held goal. If this sounds like you, you'll want to look carefully at the rankings and ratings for the colleges you're considering. Be sure to search both the college websites and websites run by independent businesses that evaluate the qualities that verify a college's claim of being outstanding. That being said, note that there is no single definition of what makes a school a "high-quality" college. For some students, it might mean the percent of graduates from that college that go on to law, medical, or other professional schools. For others, it might mean a range of exciting courses in a particular area of interest. For others, "high quality" might mean "perceived quality" or how others rank the college. But be cautious about seeking only a "name brand" college. Even though it is perfectly acceptable for students to be attuned to a college's overall excellence, prestige does not equal academic quality. Although it is appropriate to look for a strong faculty and a highly regarded college, ultimately what you want is a college where you will have the greatest chance of academic success. It is your success in college, not your school's academic reputation or prestige, that will lead to graduate school admission or a broad selection of jobs.

9. How important is "to receive a degree from a high-quality school" as a reason for my going to college?

Most Important Reason	Important Reason	Indifferent	Unimportant Reason	Least Important Reason

10. To explore the U.S. and perhaps the world

College offers an opportunity to learn about different places and the people who live there. You may choose to attend a college in a part of the country unfamiliar to you, with different types of food, customs, and attitudes. Even if you attend an in-state college, there will be opportunities to visit unfamiliar regions of the state and spend time at parks, museums, and other points of interest. Many students take advantage of college study abroad programs in order to experience a new country, language, and culture. Study abroad programs can be very affordable, usually costing about the same as a semester at college. Any international experience you can acquire will be an asset in the eyes of many employers. They are looking for graduates who have demonstrated that they can to adapt to different work styles, communicate effectively with people from various backgrounds, and successfully navigate unfamiliar terrain.

10. How important is "to explore the U.S. and perhaps the world" as a reason for my going to college?

Most Important Reason	Important Reason	Indifferent	Unimportant Reason	Least Important Reason

11. To take advantage of college life: spectator sports, clubs, activities, etc.

Like the majority of students, you may have reasons for attending college that go beyond getting a solid education. You recognize that the opportunities available both inside and outside the classroom can help you take the critical next steps into adulthood and your future career. Joining clubs and organizations develops confidence while honing essential leadership and teamwork skills. Participating in sports, either as a spectator or participant builds camaraderie and social links. For some students, "college life" may be even more important than "academic life." If that's you, you'll want a college where the academic demands will not diminish your ability to socialize. For you, your chosen school should provide a good balance between the social and educational aspects of campus life. You may want to consider schools with strong sports teams or active fraternities and sororities. Investigating what percentage of students stay on campus over the weekend will give you an idea of how strong the social culture is.

11. How important is "to take advantage of college life: spectator sports, clubs, etc." as a reason for my going to college?

Most Important Reason	Important Reason	Indifferent	Unimportant Reason	Least Important Reason

12. To get the best education possible at a reasonable cost

Most people want to use their money wisely or, in the case of most students, their parents' money. Consider whether an expensive college is worth the cost for you and your parents. There may be circumstances where shelling out big bucks for a high-priced, well-known private school is worth the investment, but it's not always the case. Yes, a college education is a significant component of improving earning potential, but the relationship between an institution's academic quality and its cost is a critical component to consider. Part of the consideration here has to do with college loans. Some families take out hundreds of thousands of dollars in loans for undergraduate education, while others don't consider an education at one particular school worth taking on a mountain of debt. When it comes to determining the value of a degree from a particular university, there are several factors to consider: the price of the school in question, the degree you are pursuing, and your earning potential once you have graduated. Weighing these factors can be difficult for students who want to follow their dreams. Someone deeply interested in the arts may find it a tough field in which to find a job, much less one that pays well. A lesson that many families are learning the hard way is that a costly degree in specific fields of study can turn into a large amount of debt and few promising job prospects.

12. How important is "to get the best education possible at a reasonable cost" as a reason for my going to college?

Most Important Reason	Important Reason	Indifferent	Unimportant Reason	Least Important Reason

Now go back and identify your top three values and circle them below.

1. To learn about different cultures, peoples, backgrounds, etc.
2. To expand my potential lifetime earnings
3. To learn essential life skills so that I can be a better parent and citizen
4. To find a vocational direction in life
5. To gain more independence and a greater sense of freedom
6. To create long-lasting relationships and professional connections.
7. To have a fresh start where no one knows me
8. To gain new skills and experiences
9. To enable me to receive a degree from a high-quality school.
10. To explore the U.S. and perhaps the world
11. To take advantage of college life: spectator sports, clubs, activities, etc.
12. To get the best education possible at a reasonable cost

Finally, in your own words, what do your top three values say about what you are looking for in a college? Has completing this exercise prompted you to think more deeply about what you want out of college and what you hope to experience there? You should write down your response to these questions and share it (and your three highest values) with your counselor, consultant, parent, or others that are helping you find a college that's good for you.

Appendix 1
Audit of College Success Traits

Name: _____

The following exercise focuses on 12 traits found to correlate with college success. The purpose of this exercise is not to provide an indelible "score" for each trait. Instead, it is designed to get you thinking about each trait in light of skills you need to succeed in college. Where you are today on the scale for each attribute is less important than where you will be when you head off to college.

Please read the full description of each trait and then indicate your level of satisfaction with how well you've incorporated this trait in your life. For example, consider Success Trait 1: Time Management. After reading the section, take a moment to think about yourself as a time manager. If you are a good time manager, you will select one of the options on the left side of the scale. If this is an area that you'd like to improve before or as you enter college, then choose one of the options on the right side of the scale. Note that each trait consists of several related components. Time management, for example, includes your ability to prioritize your time, plan ahead for assignments, and be a self-starter. You may consider yourself better in one area and weaker in another. Your task is to think of all of these components and assess how satisfied you are with your current time management traits.

There are no right or wrong responses here. Look on this as an opportunity for you to evaluate your current strengths and weaknesses and identify what traits you could work on as part of your preparation for success in college.

College Success Trait #1: Time Management

Your college experience is likely to be packed with courses, lectures, papers, maybe a part-time job on or off campus, as well as a full social life. With so much to do and so many opportunities to explore, time management is essential. In contrast to high school, where your teachers may have regularly checked in with students, in college you will not be guided in what study to do each week. Typically, there is no set of homework assignments. No one will remind you about the paper you should be researching or the course review you wanted to take. As a college student, you will be responsible for juggling all the different aspects of your life. With your education your top priority, it's crucial to devise a schedule to set specific times where you are away from other distractions and able to concentrate on studying.

Students with good time management skills have assignments that are complete, accurate, and carefully written. They do the assigned readings for their classes, and their attention to detail in the work they submit is a clear indicator of the value they place on their educational activities. They are likely to stay engaged in their studies and focused on the possible career paths ahead.

How do you envision success in college? Does success in college mean passing classes? Does it mean doing well enough to get a good job or be accepted at a great graduate school? Does it mean being a top student? You are the only who can define what success in college means to you. Whatever goals you choose to set for yourself, your path to achieving them is through good time management.

As you assess your time management abilities, consider some of these hallmarks of good time management and how many you currently practice: prioritizing time; focusing on most important tasks first; preparing a weekly schedule that includes class time, studying, activities, email, work, meals, social media time, video games, time with friends, etc.; keeping a study timetable detailing goals to achieve and target dates for reaching them; maintaining a constant, consistent, and unwavering work effort; allotting the time necessary to complete assignments without prodding; being punctual and dependable; being a self-starter; targeting clear outcomes; and planning ahead for papers and exams.

Here's how I assess my time management:

completely satisfied	very satisfied	moderately satisfied	slightly satisfied	not satisfied	I have no preference

College Success Trait #2: Study Skills

Every student who has graduated from high school student has learned a way to study. But some study methods are more effective than others.. Study skills here refer to academic abilities such as reading speed and comprehension, writing, note-taking, calculating, speaking, researching, and listening—all of which will be put to good use in your college classes. Knowing how to read efficiently, understand what you've read, take notes in class, use the library, and answer multiple-choice tests are all areas that will help you be more successful in the classroom. Students with solid study skills can also express ideas clearly, listen attentively, write clearly, and be thorough.

Good note-taking is an essential study skill because it enables you to identify and retain essential information from your college classes much more efficiently. Keep your notes in good order and review them to ensure they make sense and are easily accessible. They will be one of your greatest assets as you study for weekly quizzes and prepare for midterm and final examinations.

Here's how I assess my study skills:

completely satisfied	very satisfied	moderately satisfied	slightly satisfied	not satisfied	I have no preference

College Success Trait #3: Motivation

Motivation or drive to succeed is the most important skill you bring to college. According to studies, academic success in college correlates not with your SAT scores or high school grades but with your level of motivation. Students who are driven to succeed do succeed. Some students go to college for the fun aspects, forgetting that college is primarily an academic experience. Motivated students are clear that they are in college to learn and grow intellectually.

Motivation includes many variables—personal drive to improve and achieve; commitment to goals; initiative; readiness to act on opportunities; and optimism and resilience. When you are motivated, you are able to sustain your attention even in subjects that may seem unimportant or are unrelated to your major. Not every college course will directly relate to your future career but with motivation, you should able to find relevance in the work you are doing.

To be successful in college, you must be motivated toward your success and have confidence in yourself; you need to believe that success is possible if you make the effort. Motivation must come from within you; it must be intrinsic or self-directed. It's true that external motivators will impact your college career, but you are much more likely to succeed when your motivation comes from within. If you are self-motivated, you attend class because it helps you learn and meet your goals, not because the instructor takes attendance. You are diligent in your studies because you are driven to take advantage of all your professors and courses have to offer. You have a plan to succeed.

Here's how I assess my motivation:

completely satisfied	very satisfied	moderately satisfied	slightly satisfied	not satisfied	I have no preference

College Success Trait #4: Self-Advocacy

Self-advocacy is your ability to represent your views or interests and to recognize and speak up when you need help or support. In high school, you may have had counselors, teachers or even parents ready to step in, suggest resources, and help you resolve issues. Although you may have an advisor in college, in many situations, it's up to you to figure out how to advocate for what you need.

Being a good self-advocate means you can recognize when it's time to ask for assistance academically, socially, and personally. You are able to speak up for yourself and communicate your strengths, needs, and wishes. As a self-advocate, you take responsibility for yourself, you know your rights, and you know where to get help or who to go to with a question. You are able to communicate your needs and desires straightforwardly and without whining or anger.

The first step in self-advocacy is to determine and define your needs, strengths, and potential challenges. What stands in the way of your achieving the goals you have set for yourself? What tools and resources do you need to overcome these obstacles?

The second step is to figure out how to get what you need. You know what it is you want to accomplish, and you have a sense of what you need to make it happen. Colleges have many resources—guidance offices, academic advisors, health services—that you can turn to but you must take the first step. If you are having a problem with a class, you need to feel comfortable going to see the professor. If you have roommate problems, you will have to find the proper housing official to help you resolve the matter. If you are struggling with depression, you must be willing to seek the counseling assistance you need to feel better.

The college years are a time for learning new information, new life skills, and a new way of relating with our world. Remember that seeking help when you need it is a sign of strength and integrity, not an admission of failure.

Here's how I assess my self-advocacy:

completely satisfied	very satisfied	moderately satisfied	slightly satisfied	not satisfied	I have no preference

College Success Trait #5: Wellness Skills

Wellness skills are the actions you do to take care of your body, your emotions, and your mental health. Taking care of yourself may be even more crucial in college than in other phases of life. You're in a new environment with new challenges and a new social life. College students may sometimes feel they are invincible, but coping with unfamiliar challenges takes a toll on your physical and mental health. Stress is just as much physical as it is emotional.

Wellness means giving your body resources to manage stress and reduce the toll of emotions like anxiety or depression. Adequate sleep and a good diet can improve your mood, your athletic and classroom performance, and your ability to cope with stress. Exercise, relaxation, and good hygiene are other important aspects of self-care.

Wellness skills can include surrounding yourself with friends who support you and help you be your best self. Students with good wellness skills make smart choices, embrace low-risk options, and plan for the "what ifs" in life. They have impulse control, they play it safe, and they avoid risky behaviors.

Success in college means making the right decisions in and out of class. These decisions ultimately affect every aspect of your life—your discretionary time, study habits, predisposition to cheat, ability to take on part-time work, and success in dealing with setbacks and stress.

Here's how I assess myself on the trait of wellness skills:

completely satisfied	very satisfied	moderately satisfied	slightly satisfied	not satisfied	I have no preference

College Success Trait #6: Adaptability

Life is all about change. Some people go through transition periods with great ease while others find them more difficult. You may have already experienced some of these transitions as you moved from middle school to high school or relocated from one city to another. You may have had to deal with changes that are much harder to adapt to, such as parents divorcing or even the illness or death of a relative.

College almost always comes with big changes in everything from location, class size, and living situation to eating habits, sleep patterns, and circle of friends. Almost everyone experiences some fear and apprehension on leaving for college, but some people have more and others less skill at dealing with change. In other words, some of us are more adaptable than others.

Some time during your college years, you will be disappointed, discouraged, or maybe even derailed from your career path. How will you handle small and large setbacks such as not getting into a class you wanted to take, dealing with a troublesome roommate, or determining how to pay next year's of college tuition? Will you fall into a funk or hide from the problem using unhealthy coping strategies such as binging on food, alcohol, or social media?

Adaptable people can successfully navigate from the controlled environment of high school to the wide-open world of college. Have you met people who never seem to get sidetracked by difficulties that would bring most folks to a screeching halt? No matter what chaos the world throws at them in their career or personal life, they adapt accordingly and build a solution with the pieces they have left.

Adaptability can be found in both attitude and action. Adaptable people learn from their mistakes rather than lament them. They ask questions, seek out mentors, and respond to obstacles by coming up with diverse and creative ways to overcome them. Adaptable people plan. They know that everyone experiences setbacks in life so they're accustomed to coming up with ideas or alternatives to try.

Here's how I assess myself on the trait of adaptability:

completely satisfied	very satisfied	moderately satisfied	slightly satisfied	not satisfied	I have no preference

College Success Trait #7: Even-Temperedness

Even-tempered people are calm, steady, and in control of their emotions. They tend to be skilled at managing relationships, resolving conflicts, and finding ways to collaborate with others. They keep things in perspective, roll with the punches, and accept change as a part of life.

Students who are even-tempered are typically adept at handling stress, boredom, anxiety, or disappointment. They tend to have better relationships with teachers and peers, which has a positive effect on their academic performance and their college experience. If a specific goal or ideal becomes unattainable due an adverse situation or unforeseen event, even-tempered students accept circumstances that cannot be changed and focus on actions that they can take. They usually maintain a hopeful outlook, and their optimism empowers them to expect that good things will happen to them

Here's how I assess myself on the trait of even-temperedness:

completely satisfied	very satisfied	moderately satisfied	slightly satisfied	not satisfied	I have no preference

College Success Trait #8: Resourcefulness

Resourcefulness is the ability to make do with what you have, see possibilities that others might not see, and anticipate the challenges you encounter in college. In a time saturated with quick fixes and easy solutions, resourceful folks stand out for their willingness to look beyond the facile or expected option. People with resourceful friends are often in awe of their problem-solving skills, not realizing that with practice they could strengthen their own resourcefulness.

Being resourceful means knowing how to solve problems. It includes the ability to take in the big picture or many sides of a problem, the tenacity to not give up when issues get complicated, and the maturity to learn from mistakes made along the way. There are three key parts to successful problem-solving:
- Understand or define the problem.
- Devise a plan to resolve the problem.
- Carry out the plan to resolve the problem.

Resourceful students are information gatherers. They seek answers to a problem or people who have information they can use to find a solution. Confronted by a research paper that needs writing, resourceful students track down appropriate books, websites, and other resources. They use search engines like Google quickly and successfully. A college campus offers countless resources such as academic advising; counseling/personal guidance; financial aid and scholarship info; tutoring; library services; health center; career and employment services; accessibility/disability resources; multicultural centers; clubs, activities, and sports offices; services for specific student groups; information technology services; and, of course, faculty office hours. Resourceful students take the time to learn about these supports and utilize them. They prove the adage "Success is not about your resources. It's about how resourceful you are with what you have."

Here's how I assess myself on the trait of resourcefulness:

completely satisfied	very satisfied	moderately satisfied	slightly satisfied	not satisfied	I have no preference

College Success Trait #9: Social Fluency

College is a social experience, both inside and outside the lecture hall. Interacting with others on campus is essential to getting the most out of your college experience. Socially fluent students are good at meeting people and establishing friendships. They are sensitive and caring and find it easy to develop rapport with faculty members and other students. Social fluent students get out of their college dorm rooms! They join organizations, do volunteer work, participate in sports, and try out for plays.

On a college campus, students are often called upon to work in groups where teamwork and collaboration are required. Residence halls, clubs, and other groups are essentially communities of individuals who come and go. Socially fluent students are able to successfully navigate these sometimes turbulent social waters. Although they can work productively in a group, they are also able to confront someone when necessary. They are often skilled listeners, negotiators, mediators, and motivators.

Socially fluent people find mentors in college—a professor, coach, dean, upper-class student, or even an off-campus employer. In high school, your teachers are expected to look out for you and lend a helping hand or a shoulder to cry on when you need it. While you don't need this support any less in college, you should assume that the burden of finding the support lies with you. It's up to you to take the initiative and find individuals who can give you support and advice, as well as a kick in the pants when you need it!

Introducing yourself to faculty members and getting to know them is always a good idea. You never know when you'll have questions about assignments, tests, or course material. When you are more than just a name on the roster, professors are better able to provide you with guidance about your major or future career or write recommendation letters for a job or graduate school.

An essential part of social fluency is networking. Students who network well are open to making new friends and building relationships and can communicate effectively with other students, faculty, and administrators. Research shows that when students connect to peers or mentors, they tend to stick to their commitments and follow through. Often the students who fail to graduate or are unsuccessful in college are those who have not taken the time to engage with others outside of class or were reluctant to explore activities involving new people. When these students get stuck or encounter obstacles, they lack a support system made up of friends, teachers, coaches, and counselors. There is no one to hold them accountable or urge them to keep going.

Here's how I assess myself on the trait of social fluency:

completely satisfied	very satisfied	moderately satisfied	slightly satisfied	not satisfied	I have no preference

College Success Trait #10: Intercultural/Interracial/Global Curiosity

In today's higher education, diversity is more than just a buzzword. Universities worldwide are pushing for more diverse student bodies and faculties and are creating programs to encourage more people from underrepresented groups to enter higher learning. A diverse student body and faculty can open the door to broader and more rigorous discussions, and ultimately, lead to better and more robust ideas.

Most large universities are already diverse spaces. Students are of different ages, different races and religions, different sexual orientation, and different educational backgrounds. They come from different socioeconomic groups and geographic areas—cities, rural areas—and even from different nations. With all this diversity, colleges and universities offer you a unique opportunity to learn from and about other people.

In order to learn from these differences, however, you need to be curious and open to listening to the opinions and beliefs of others, even when these opinions and beliefs differ from yours. The more curious you are, the more you will want to examine assumptions, correct misunderstandings, acknowledge history and context, display inclusivity, navigate cultural norms tactfully, and even confront prejudice and discrimination.

Here's how I assess myself on the trait of intercultural/interracial/global curiosity:

completely satisfied	very satisfied	moderately satisfied	slightly satisfied	not satisfied	I have no preference

College Success Trait #11: Assertiveness

Assertiveness is the ability to express your feelings, opinions, beliefs, and needs directly, openly, and honestly while not violating the personal rights of others. When properly conducted, assertive communication can lead to respectful dialogue. Assertiveness skills are helpful in roommate communication, study groups, teams, and conflict resolution. Successful college students are assertive. They speak up for themselves and for other people; they speak out when someone tries to take advantage of them or others.

An assertive person does not need to be domineering, aggressive, or overbearing. Assertiveness does not call for yelling, demanding, name-calling, or putting down others. Any of those scenarios are likely to end with the other person feeling disrespected, attacked, and defensive. On the other hand, not sharing your feelings may be interpreted as "passive" or non-assertive. The other person may feel excluded from both the opportunity to understand your feelings and respond to your concerns. Assertive communication by all involved parties is the preferred approach for successful communication.

In any situation calling for assertiveness on your part, you want to be transparent, honest, and open about your feelings, opinions, and needs. Do not let your friends, classmates, or others impose or force their behaviors, values, and ideas on you. Let them know where you stand, what you think, how you feel, and what you want. You are always allowed to say no to unreasonable requests. Use the word "no" and explain why only if you choose.

Here's how I assess myself on the trait of assertiveness

completely satisfied	very satisfied	moderately satisfied	slightly satisfied	not satisfied	I have no preference

College Success Trait #12: Resiliency

College life includes peaks and valleys, occasions of great joy as well as setbacks and disappointments. Individuals with resiliency have a mental reservoir of strength that can carry them through troubled times.

Psychologists define resilience as the process of adapting well in the face of adversity, tragedy, threats, or other significant sources of stress, family and relationship problems, health issues, or other stressors. As much as resilience involves "bouncing back" from difficult experiences, it can also lead to major personal growth. While adverse events can be painful and difficult, they don't have to determine the outcome of your college career. In most aspects of your college life, you can control, modify, and grow with defeat. Being more resilient not only helps you get through challenging circumstances but also empowers you to grow and even improve your life.

Resilient people also tend to communicate well, hold favorable views of themselves and their abilities, possess the capacity to make realistic plans and stick to them, and see themselves as fighters rather than victims.

Here's how I assess myself on the trait of resiliency:

completely satisfied	very satisfied	moderately satisfied	slightly satisfied	not satisfied	I have no preference

Appendix J
References for College Planning

In addition to the listings provided here, additional resources, including websites, are cited throughout this book, most particularly in **Chapters 4** and **5**.

Comprehensive Guidebooks and Websites

ACT (act.org)

Barron's Profiles of American Colleges (www.barronspac.com)

College Board and Big Future (collegeboard.org; bigfuture.org)

College Data (collegedata.com)

College Navigator: National Center for Education Statistics (nces.ed.gov/collegenavigator; major database college information.)

College Results (collegeresults.org)

Council of Public Liberal Arts Colleges (coplac.org)

Education Planner (educationplanner.org)

Integrated Postsecondary Education Data System: National Center for Education Statistics (nces.ed.gov/ipeds)

National Association of Independent Colleges and Universities (ucan-network.org)

National Collegiate Honors Council (nchchonors.org)

Peterson's Four-Year Colleges

Peterson's Two-Year Colleges

Public University Honors (publicuniversityhonors.com)

Application Process

Admission Matters: What Students and Parents Need to Know About Getting into College, Springer, Sally P.; Reider, Jon; and Morgan, Joyce Vining

Coalition for College Application (coalitionforcollegeaccess.org/)

College Board and Big Future (collegeboard.org; bigfuture.org; the site of one of the two major testing companies.)

College Scorecard (collegescorecard.ed.gov; US Department of Education interactive tool for college and cost information.)

Common Application (commonapp.org)

Common Black College Application (commonblackcollegeapp.com/)

Common Data Set (search "Common Data Set, x college"; official admissions and enrollment information.)

Complete College Planner, Princeton Review

DIY College Rankings (diycollegerankings.com)

FairTest (fairtest.org; in addition to schools that are test optional, resources on broad
    test issues.)
Gatekeepers, Steinberg, Jacques
Professor Pathfinder's U.S. College and University Reference Map, Hedberg Maps, Inc.
Social media sites for colleges
Truth about College Admissions, Barnard, B. and Clark, R.
Who Get in and Why, Selingo, Jeffrey

Subjective Reviews

Alumni Factor (alumnifactor.com; college rankings based on graduate success)
America's Best Colleges for B Students, Orr, Tamra
Barron's Profiles of American Colleges (www.barronspac.com)
Best Colleges, The Princeton Review
Best Value Colleges (Princeton Review online)
Blogs, student (check on college website)
Cappex (cappex.com)
College Finder, Antonoff, Steven R.
College Vine (collegevine.com)
*Colleges That Change Lives: 40 Schools That Will Change the Way You Think About
    Colleges*, Pope, Loren (Oswald, Hilary M., editor)
CollegeXpress (collegexpress.com)
*Cool Colleges: For the Hyper-Intelligent, Self-Directed, Late Blooming, and Just Plain
    Different*, Asher, Donald
Fiske Guide to Colleges, Fiske, Edward B.
Good University Guide (UK universities)
Hispanic Serving Institutions in Practice by Garcia, Gina Ann
Inside Honors: Ratings and Reviews of Sixty Public University Honors Programs,
    Willingham, John
MacLean's Guide To Canadian Universities
        (macleans.ca/education-hub/build-your-own-university-ranking/)
Niche (niche.com)
Other College Guide, Sweetland, Jane; Glastris, Paul; and the Staff of Washington Monthly
Parchment (parchment.com)
Social media channels (Facebook, LinkedIn, etc.) (check colleges by name)
Ultimate Guide to America's Best Colleges, Tanabe, Gen and Tanabe, Kelly
Unigo (unigo.com; reviews and tools to aid in college selection)
US News and World Report (usnews.com/education) (highly subjective ranking system)
YouTube (search name of college and "university campus tour")

College Costs and Financial Aid

Affordable Colleges Online
(https://www.affordablecollegesonline.org/financial-aid/college-calculators/)

Best Value Colleges (Princeton Review online)

Best Value Colleges, Kiplinger (kiplinger.com/tool/college/T014-S001-kiplinger-s-best-values-in-public-colleges/index.php)

College cost calculator (https://www.calculator.net/college-cost-calculator.html)

College Cost Navigator (collegecostnavigator.com)

College Solution (thecollegesolution.com)

Colleges Worth Your Money, Belasco, Andrew, Bergman, Dave, and Trivette, Michael

Edvisors (edvisors.com)

FAFSA4caster and Federal Student Aid (studentaid.ed.gov; estimates of eligibility for Federal Student Aid.)

Fast Web (fastweb.com; online scholarship search)

Federal Student Aid/U.S. Department of Education (fafsa.ed.gov; includes FAFSA4caster to check aid eligibility)

Financial Aid (finaid.org; created by Mark Kantrowitz, financial aid author)

Getting Financial Aid, College Board

Hispanic Scholarship Consortium (hispanicscholar.org)

How to Control Your College Costs, Law, Claire

National Association of Student Financial Aid Administrators
(http://www.nasfaa.org/Students_Parents_Counselors); site of organization of financial aid administrators.)

Net price calculator (search name of college and "net price calculator")

Paying for College, Princeton Review and Kalman Chany.

Saving for College (savingforcollege.com) (particularly helpful with 529 plans and planning ahead for college costs)

The Price You Pay for College, Ron Lieber

Twisdoms About Paying for College, Kantrowitz, Mark

Ultimate Scholarship Book, Tanabe, Gen and Kelly

Topical Resources

American Gap Association (americangap.org)

Applerouth Testing (applerouth.com) (test prep business company with free resources)

Best Summer Programs for Teens: America's Top Classes, Camps, and Courses for College-Bound Students, Berger, Sandra

Better College Essay, Stone, Elizabeth and Charlson, M.

Christian Guide to Christian Colleges and Universities, North American Coalition for Christian Admission Professions (naccap.org)

College Essay Essentials, Sawyer, Ethan

Compass Education Group (compassprep.com/testing-videos/) (test prep company with
 practice tests)
Fraternities and Sororities (greekpages.com)
HBCU's http://www.thehundred-seven.org/hbculist.html
Hillel International Guide to Jewish Life on Campus (hillel.org/college-guide)
Hispanic Outlook in Higher Education Magazine (hispanicoutlook.com)
How Is College Different From High School? (https://www.smu.edu/provost/sasp/
 NeatStuffforNewStudents/HowIsCollegeDifferentfromHighSchool)
Naked Roommate: And 107 Other Issues You Might Run Into In College, Cohen, Harlan
Newman Connection (newmanconnection.com)
Newman Society Guide to Catholic Colleges
 (cardinalnewmansociety.org/TheNewmanGuide.aspx)
Times Good University Guide, O'Leary, John (colleges in the United Kingdom)
Ultimate Guide to College Transfer: From Surviving to Thriving, Tyler, L. and Henninger, S.
Universities and Colleges Admissions Service (UCAS.com; application for admission to
 colleges in the United Kingdom)

Diversity, Inclusion and First Generation

Campus Pride (campuspride.org)
College Equity Index (collegeequityfirst.org)
Consortium of Higher Education/LGBT Resource Professionals (lgbtcampus.org; click on
 "Find an LGBTQA Campus Center")
Educators for Fair Consideration (E4FC.org; first generation/undocumented students)
Hispanic Association of Colleges and Universities (hacu.net)
Hispanic Outlook in Higher Education Magazine (hispanicoutlook.com)
Historically Black Colleges and Universities (hbcuconnect.com)
I'm First Guide to College (imfirst.org; first generation)

Majors, Academic Programs, and Careers

Carleton College Career Paths (apps.carleton.edu/career/visualize)
College Completion (collegecompletion.chronicle.com; graduation rates, percent of students
 on Pell grants.)
College Results (collegeresults.org; information about college graduation rates.)
Creative Colleges: A Guide for Student Actors, Artists, Dancers, Musicians and Writers,
 Loveland, Elaina
Educate to Career (educatetocareer.org; return on investment college listings.)
Guide to Writing Programs, Association of Writers and Writing Programs
 (https://www.awpwriter.org/guide/guide_writing_programs)
Impact of Major on Career Path for 15,600 Williams College Alums
 (https://web.williams.edu/Mathematics/devadoss/careerpath.html)

National Directory of College Athletics (collegiatedirectories.com)

O*Net (onetonline.org; occupation search)

What Color is Your Parachute for Teens, Christen, Carol and Bolles, Richard

Where You Go is Not Who You'll Be, Bruni, Frank

Learning Disabilities

Children and Adults with Attention-Deficit/Hyperactivity Disorder (chadd.org)

College Supports for Learning Differences (CSLD) (collegesupports.com; online guide to
college support services for students with LD, ADHD, and Autism Spectrum disorders)

CollegeWebLD (collegewebld.com; "helped thousands of students with learning differences
find a college that fits their unique needs)

*K&W Guide to College Programs and Services for Students with Learning Disabilities or
Attention Deficit/Hyperactivity Disorder*, Princeton Review, Kravets, M. and Wax, I.

Landmark College (landmark.edu/research-training/ld-resources; (a college for students
with learning differences offers online resources)

LD OnLine (ldonline.org; resources and advice on learning differences/disabilities)

Learning Disabilities Association of America (ldaamerica.org)

Nonverbal Learning Disabilities Project (nvld.org) identifies key components for students
with learning and attention issues and focus on when they enter college.

Parent Resources

College Parent Central (collegeparentcentral.com; advice, reviews, etc.)

College Parents of America (collegeparents.org; general support, travel discounts)

College Ready: Expert Advice for Parents to Simplify the College Transition,
Petree, C., editor

College Success Guaranteed 2.0: 5 Rules for Parents, Gauld, Malcolm

College Wellness Guide, Princeton Review and Franek, Robert.

Greatest College Health Guide, Henry, Jill and Henry, Dave.

Grown and Flown (grownandflown.com) (parenting, off to college, etc.)

*How to Raise an Adult: Break Free of the Overparenting Trap and Prepare Your Kid for
Success*, Lythcott-Haims, Julie

Letting Go: A Parent's Guide to Understanding the College Years, Coburn, Karen L. and
Treeger, Madge L.

Search Institute Developmental Assets (https://www.search-institute.org/our-research/
development-assets/)

*Wired and Connected: Brain-Based Solution to ensure your child's social and emotional
success*, Knippenberg, C.

Interesting and Related

Am I There Yet? The Loop-de-Loop, Zigzagging Journey to Adulthood, Andrew, Mari

Character Collaborative (character-admission.org)

Defining Decade: Why Your Twenties Matter by Jay, Meg

Gratitude Project edited by Smith, Jeremy, Newman, Kira, Marsh, Jason, Keltner, Dacher

Grit: The Power of Passion and Perseverance, Duckworth, Angela.

Making the Most of College, Light, Richard

Mindset: The New Psychology of Success, Dweck, Carol S.

Paradox of Choice, Schwartz, Barry

Wildhood, Natterson-Horowitz, Barbara, and Bowers, Kathryn

About the Author
Steven R. Antonoff

For almost 40 years, Steven R. Antonoff has built his knowledge of effective ways to assist students in finding colleges where students can thrive and be happy. Over those years, he has also built his knowledge of colleges and universities themselves. As an independent educational consultant, Dr. Antonoff has worked with several thousand students and has visited (and revisited) hundreds of colleges. He has also played a key role in shaping the profession of independent educational consulting, developing certification standards, and creating and teaching a curriculum for the field.

In addition to **College Match**, Dr. Antonoff is the author of **The College Finder: Choosing the School That's Right for You**. Since 1993, and now in its fourth edition, **College Finder** has been a go-to source for helping students and college counselors build college lists.

Dr. Antonoff is also the author of **A Student of Colleges: Fundamentals of Independent Educational Consulting**. The book is a textbook for college consultants, including college affordability, building a college list, learning disabilities, counseling strategies, and knowledge acquisition. It is the first textbook written for professionals in this field.

His writings have led to popular tools for students to use in their college planning. For example, students widely use the "Self-Survey for the College Bound" through school and independent counselor offices to help them learn more about traits and characteristics useful in exploring colleges. Similar tools, measuring different features, are analyzed via the "College Planning Values Assessment" and "Audit of College Success Traits." Antonoff's work includes additional student surveys concerning identifying the factors pertinent to college planning, college visit evaluation strategies, and ways to compare colleges. Barron's Profiles of American Colleges has included Dr. Antonoff's article and assessment, "Know Yourself," for almost 20 years. He has also authored surveys for use by admission planning professionals.

A popular speaker and webinar presenter, Dr. Antonoff has covered a wide range of topics. Session titles include: "Using Surveys in College Consulting," The Best Resources for the Independent Educational Consultant," "Ranking the Academic Quality of Colleges," "Parents and College Planning," "Solving the College Admission Puzzle," "College Shopping: Getting in and Fitting in," "The World Is Flat and Only Ivy League Colleges Are Good: Myth, Reality and Wisdom in College Planning," "College Admission—Separating Fact from Fiction," "Lifelong Learning Opportunities," "The High-Maintenance Parent," "A Career in Independent Educational Consulting," "Building a College List with Confidence," and "College Planning: De-stressing or Distressing?".

In the Independent Educational Consultant Association (IECA), Dr Antonoff was president of the board of directors; member of the Executive Committee; and chair of the nominating committee, long-range planning committee, education and training committee, college committee, and strategic planning committee. In addition, Dr. Antonoff chaired the search committee to hire the association's current CEO. Instrumental in founding the IECA Summer Training Institute, Dr. Antonoff has served on the faculty for nearly two decades.

He served as chair of the board of trustees of the IECA Foundation (iecafoundation.org), the charitable arm of the professional consulting association. The Foundation supports programs that have a significant impact on students and their educational environments. It has given grants totaling over $350,000 since 2003. Priority is given to programs that assist students as they make educational choices. It provides assistance to small, lesser-known programs and projects that produce pragmatic, measurable results for young people whose needs are often unmet.

Dr. Antonoff is an instructor and member of the advisory board for the certificate program in independent educational consulting through the University of California, Irvine (UCI). He previously taught educational consulting courses through the University of California, Los Angeles (UCLA) college counseling program. His former students are independent educational consultants and college counselors, practicing both nationally and abroad. Dr. Antonoff also chaired the five-year evaluation of the UCI certificate program.

Dr. Antonoff is the founding chair of the commission on credentialing of the American Institute for Certified Educational Planners. The commission grants the CEP designation to those who demonstrate advanced consulting skills and pass a board-certified assessment.

Dr. Antonoff is a member of the Higher Education Consultants Association and the National Association for College Admission Counseling (NACAC). He has consulted with the International Baccalaureate Latino Association at a Denver high school. He has also served on the NACAC by-laws revision task force.

Dr. Antonoff was the first recipient of the IECA Professional Achievement Award, created to recognize contributions to the profession of independent educational consulting. The award, now called the Steven R. Antonoff Award for Professional Achievement, is presented annually.

Before becoming an independent educational consultant, Dr. Antonoff spent 11 years in college administration, serving as dean of admissions and financial aid, executive director of admissions and student affairs, and dean of students at the University of Denver. At 22, he was one of the youngest Deans of Students in the country. He earned an undergraduate degree in psychology from Colorado State University and a master's degree in education, and a Ph.D. in human communication studies from the University of Denver. Beyond professional pursuits, Antonoff was chair of the City of Denver's Commission on the Arts and served as chair of the board of the Denver Hospice.

By Dr. Steven R. Antonoff

The College Finder: Choosing the School That's Right for You!
College Match: A Blueprint for Choosing the Best School for You
A Student of Colleges: Fundamentals of Independent Educational Consulting

College Match, is available on Amazon and www.EDUconsultingMedia.com

Write to info@EDUconsultingMedia.com to inquire about bulk discounts, school examination copies, and signed copies. Dr. Antonoff's website is www.schoolbuff.com.

Acknowledgments

An author owes so much to those who support their writing. I have felt that support for almost three decades. I am very thankful to my very faithful readers for trusting me to provide guidance into the college search process and for referring this book to friends and relatives. I am particularly grateful to the schools that have adopted the book as a text in college counseling classes and programs.

College Match was inspired by the hundreds of students with whom I've worked. They helped immeasurably in the preparation of these pages. Every worksheet has benefited from their careful reading and assessment. But, more importantly, each student has, in their own way, opened my eyes to another issue, another possibility, another frame of reference involved in college choice. I have learned from each of them.

Authors know how important editors are to their work, and that is certainly true of me. Editors not only read line-by-line for the basics but also for clarity and flow of ideas. My editor, Maripat Murphy, made useful and essential suggestions and changes. In addition to her expertise with grammar, consistency, and such, Maripat is also a terrific researcher. As often as the copy was checked and rechecked, Maripat triple-checked and often caught errors I missed. She is effective for many reasons, including her curiosity about the college admission process and because she went through this process with her daughter. While she preserved my voice, her expertise is reflected on each of these pages.

This edition of Match continues to benefit from the art of Milan Glosic. For the first time, it includes a cover drawn completely by Milan. He also contributed chapter and other illustrations. I appreciate his continued efforts to make the book more accessible.

My research assistants relied on Zoom and email through the pandemic to double-check information and links included. Caroline Nellis and Georgia Grace Armatas contributed significant portions of Chapters 4 and 5, respectively. I'm also grateful for the work of Julia Dykstra, Ivan Ramirez-Munoz and Johan Dellgren. I enjoy this supplemental opportunity to work with high school and college students—and recent graduates.

Adding visual touches to a book and making the pages appealing (and readable!) are often taken for granted. The new design of this edition of College Match showcases the talents of Erika Gritters of I/O Designs, Littleton, Colorado. She helped make the text and the worksheets user-friendly. I am grateful for her creativity, energy, and hard work.

For this edition, many of the worksheets and surveys have been revised, some quite dramatically. Among other numerical manipulations, I needed help with factor analysis.

Miriam Cummings helped with these analyses. Miriam is a Ph.D. candidate at the University of Colorado, Denver, studying education research and evaluation methods. Her work is most on display in Worksheet 1, the Self-Survey for the College Bound. Miriam analyzed several thousand surveys taken by students over the years, and her work resulted in new survey questions and updated categories. Miriam also greatly assisted in the revisions of Appendix F and Appendix G.

Continued thanks are due to Dr. Marie Friedemann, my coauthor on the earliest editions of College Match. So many of Marie's concepts and perspectives live on in these pages—and will for as long as the book exists. Her sensitivity toward students, her keen eye and ear for college planning issues, and her clean, active writing style are at the heart of this book. Marie remains a colleague and a friend. Any success of College Match is a tribute to her efforts.

My appreciation also goes to the many independent educational consultants and high school college counselors who continue to use the book and share insights and perspectives. More directly, their suggestions enhanced the clarity and functionality of the College Match worksheets. Being a college advisor can be difficult, stressful, and time-consuming, and their resolute efforts on behalf of young people are acknowledged here